Jumpstart UIKit

Learn to Build Enterprise-Level, Feature-Rich Websites that Work Elegantly with Minimum Fuss

Aravind Shenoy

Apress®

Jumpstart UIKit

Aravind Shenoy
Mumbai, Maharashtra, India

ISBN-13 (pbk): 978-1-4842-6028-9   ISBN-13 (electronic): 978-1-4842-6029-6
https://doi.org/10.1007/978-1-4842-6029-6

Copyright © 2020 by Aravind Shenoy

Managing Director, Apress Media LLC: Welmoed Spahr
Acquisitions Editor: Louise Corrigan
Development Editor: James Markham
Coordinating Editor: Nancy Chen

Cover designed by eStudioCalamar

Cover image designed by Freepik (www.freepik.com)

Distributed to the book trade worldwide by Springer Science+Business Media New York, 1 New York Plaza, New York, NY 10004. Phone 1-800-SPRINGER, fax (201) 348-4505, e-mail orders-ny@springer-sbm.com, or visit www.springeronline.com. Apress Media, LLC is a California LLC and the sole member (owner) is Springer Science + Business Media Finance Inc (SSBM Finance Inc). SSBM Finance Inc is a **Delaware** corporation.

For information on translations, please e-mail booktranslations@springernature.com; for reprint, paperback, or audio rights, please e-mail bookpermissions@springernature.com.

Apress titles may be purchased in bulk for academic, corporate, or promotional use. eBook versions and licenses are also available for most titles. For more information, reference our Print and eBook Bulk Sales web page at http://www.apress.com/bulk-sales.

Any source code or other supplementary material referenced by the author in this book is available to readers on GitHub via the book's product page, located at www.apress.com/9781484260289. For more detailed information, please visit http://www.apress.com/source-code.

Printed on acid-free paper

*I dedicate this book to my uncle **Ramanath N. Kamath**, who has been my rock since childhood. Also, heartfelt gratitude to **Professor Dange**, an ex-IIT mentor, who guided me on the Theory of Machines and laid a solid foundation for my perception about engineering and technology 20 years ago.*

Table of Contents

About the Author ix

About the Technical Reviewer xi

Acknowledgments xiii

Chapter 1: QuickStart UIkit 1

   Evolution of Responsive Web Design 1

      Responsive vs. Adaptive Web Design 3

   Getting Started with UIkit...5

      Installing UIkit...7

   Summary...12

      References 12

Chapter 2: Grid System, Containers, and Helper Classes 13

   UIkit Starter Template 14

   Flexbox-Powered Grid Layout 16

      Grids and Width 16

   Containers..41

   Utility Classes..45

      Floats..45

      Border Radius..46

      Drop Cap...50

      Logo..51

   Summary..53

Chapter 3: Navigation Elements and Media Attributes.......................55

Navigation..55

    Dropdown..56

    List Navigations..61

    Tabs..66

    Navbar..70

    Breadcrumbs..77

    Icon Navigation..79

    Sub Navigation...81

    Thumbnail Navigation..83

Media Attributes..87

    Labels...87

    Badges..88

    Carousels..89

    Slideshow...95

Summary...102

Chapter 4: Active CSS and JavaScript Components 103

Buttons..104

    Normal Buttons..104

    Contextual-Colored Buttons...105

    Different-Sized Buttons...106

    Button Width Modifiers...107

    Grouped Buttons..108

Icons...109

    Normal Icons..110

    Icons with Ratio Modifiers..110

    Social Media Icons...112

Accordions 113

Alerts...116

Tooltips..120

Modals 122

    Normal Modals 122

    Full-Width Modals 125

    Image Modals 127

Panels 128

Tiles...131

Upload 135

Inverse 137

Visibility...140

Pagination 143

Animations 146

Transition 150

Summary...153

Chapter 5: Forms and Tables 155

Forms...155

    Simple Input Textbox 156

    Contextual Colored-Form Textboxes..157

    Grid-Width Input Textboxes...161

    Select Options 162

    Icons within Textboxes 164

    Forms with Stacked Labels 166

    Sign-Up Form 169

Tables...172

Summary...185

Chapter 6: Web Design - Peek into the Upcoming Trends in 2020 187

Animations, Extensive Use of Colors, and Eye-Catching Typography 188

Mobile-Friendly Design 189

Progressive Web Apps 189

Agile Design Practices and Data-Driven Design 190

Flat Design 191

Emergence of Single-Page Websites 191

Organic Illustrations 192

Chat-bots 192

Accessibility 193

Voice Search 193

Summary 195

Index 197

About the Author

A senior content writer by profession, **Aravind Shenoy's** core interests are technical writing, content writing, content development, web design, and business analysis. He was born and raised in Mumbai and currently resides there. A music buff - he loves listening to Rock n' Roll and Rap. Oasis, R.E.M, The Doors, Dire Straits, Coldplay, Jimi Hendrix, 3 Doors Down, Chemical Brothers, U2, Guns n' Roses, and Michael Jackson rule his playlists. An engineering graduate from the Manipal Institute of Technology and an author of several books, he is a keen learner and believes that there is always a steep learning curve as Life is all about learning. In summary, as he quips, "The most important thing is to be happy - it's all that matters. After all, we are here for a good time, not a long time."

About the Technical Reviewer

Anselm Bradford is a front-end web developer passionate about open source projects for government, nonprofits, and higher education.

Currently, he is developing tools to help protect consumers from misleading and illegal financial practices. He has experience working on social services discovery for Code for America, user research at Imgur, and digital media curriculum development at Auckland University of Technology.

Anselm is the lead author on the book *HTML5 Mastery* (Apress, 2011).

Acknowledgments

*I would like to thank the entire team at Apress, including Louise; Nancy; Jim; and specifically the technical reviewer, **Anselm Bradford**, for their exemplary work on this 12th book of mine. It has indeed been awesome collaborating with them on this book, and their efforts mean a lot when it comes to making this book a success.*

A special thanks to my sister Aruna, too, remembering our childhood times, and for tolerating my idiosyncrasies while growing up.

CHAPTER 1

QuickStart UIkit

UIkit is a lightweight web design framework with modular components that help you rapidly design robust user interfaces. It comes with a slew of ready-to-use elements like cards, buttons, and navigation helpers among other power-packed utilities to build clean and fully functional web pages. Responsive by default, it removes the guesswork out of developing mobile-friendly layouts in a minimalistic way. The set of tools that is ingrained in this front-end framework is quite simple to use, customize, and extend. It enables you to create consistent feature-rich sites, without the bloat or clutter associated with popular heavyweight frameworks like Bootstrap and Foundation.

Before we take our first steps in UIkit, let's look at the evolution of responsive web design.

Evolution of Responsive Web Design

Web design initially started with sites built for a screen size. As a result, the output resulted in web pages optimized for that device/screen size only. When the resulting output was viewed on smaller or wider screens, it looked inappropriate in terms of readability, aesthetics, and usability. The layout showed congested content on smaller screens and excessive whitespace on larger screens. This led to a shabby user experience when designers attempted to present more information on the web page.

© Aravind Shenoy 2020
A. Shenoy, *Jumpstart UIKit*, https://doi.org/10.1007/978-1-4842-6029-6_1

Apart from a fixed width, the other alternative approach during that era was liquid design wherein the web pages would flow and stretch depending on the browser space. However, designers had to compromise on aesthetics due to the irregular display of content and excessive whitespace. In addition, this caused usability issues. More so, the elastic nature of the output made designing quite difficult. The guesswork resulted in designers performing innumerable testing procedures just to get the basic view right.

With the massive technological advances in mobile phones, more users started using the mobile platform. Then a new trend began with web designers creating two sites: one for the desktop and the other for the mobile phone with different URLs (read *Web Addresses*). Multiple sites caused usability issues as end users expected the mobile platform to display all the attributes and features found in the desktop version of the site.

There was a crucial requirement for flexible methodologies that could ensure a satisfying user experience across both the mobile as well as the desktop site versions. Resolution-dependent layout seemed more like the need of the hour. However, this meant that web designers had to use a lot of tedious JavaScript code to fix the resulting web pages on different platforms, based on the screen resolution.

It was then that the seeds of responsive web design were sown. Initially, the concepts were quite obscure - ultimately, they narrowed down to the use of Fluid Grids, Fluid Images, and Media Queries. Subsequently, Media Queries were decisive in addressing the fluidity processes required for site optimization across multiple platforms as they enabled building efficient layouts using CSS rather than complicated JavaScript code. Responsive web design then started becoming a norm for website development. Responsive web design is device- and screen-size agnostic - meaning it creates a seamless user experience on mobile or desktop platforms without too much compromise on varying factors like usability, performance, functionality, and aesthetics, just to mention a few. Moreover, it abstracted the need to create multiple site versions for the desktop as well as mobile phones. Modern layouts include diverse approaches such as Multi-columns, FlexBox, and Grids, which empowered the responsive web design paradigm.

In the coming years, the rapid rise of mobile technologies resulted in smartphones becoming the preferred media for accessing or browsing the information on the web. Soon, a mobile-first paradigm became the de facto norm. Mobile-first design involves building a website/app for the mobile platform. Once the site has been designed, it is tweaked for the bigger screens/bigger devices like tablets, desktops, or large display screens. It is all about creating an immersive user experience on smartphones and other small-screen mobile devices. If the majority of your users are mobile users, then this approach will be optimal. Also, it is tailored to fill all the gaps specifically for mobile devices but may lack in certain aspects when it comes to traditional desktop site versions.

Coming back to responsive web design, user experience is the pivotal factor. You need to create and develop a site that will consider usability and user environment as the focal points. Responsive web design not only makes site design faster but also delivers on the uniformity and code maintenance fronts.

In the next section, we will learn about Responsive vs. Adaptive web design in brief and the varying concepts associated with them.

Responsive vs. Adaptive Web Design

Responsive web design is an intuitive approach where the layout dynamically alters depending on the screen size and orientation. Responsive web design is a good choice if you are building a website from scratch. But it can be a quite complex process as the site has to fit into every device window and resolution. More than aesthetics, usability is an imperative concern in responsive design. Nowadays, the complexities related to responsive design have reduced significantly due to a plethora of visually appealing, effective themes, which can be used with popular content management systems (CMS) such as WordPress and Drupal.

Adaptive web design is slightly different from responsive design as it loads static layouts based on the respective screen size. In adaptive design, breakpoints are used for defining multiple viewports. The most common practice in adaptive design methodology is developing based on the following screen widths, namely - 320, 480, 760, 960, 1200, and 1600. However, this is just a popular approach, meaning you can design it for more viewports than the preceding screen sizes.

Both responsive and adaptive web design concepts come with their high points and low points. In responsive layouts, the site speed is slower as the layout changes dynamically in accordance with the device/browser window. Also, due to this type of elasticity, there is less control over how the content restructures and is eventually displayed on the screen.

In adaptive design, due to static layouts, the page loading times are quicker. In addition, you have more control over the content as you can optimize layouts for a particular screen-width setting or user group much better. Gaining actionable and meaningful insights using analytics, you can determine the site layout that gets the maximum hits. Lesser bounce rates and satisfying user experiences have been observed in adaptive layouts compared to responsive layouts - mainly as you can build powerful layouts catering to a specific user base or user preferences.

Scalability, code upkeep, testing, and upgrades/updates in adaptive design can be tedious as you have to modify and manage several layouts compared to a single layout in responsive design. Moreover, responsive sites are more SEO friendly.

In traditional desktop sites, users are accustomed to a specific look, feel, and usability quotient. However, you may need to overhaul these websites in line with the current trends and upcoming technologies. In such cases that need retrofitting, adaptive design is quite useful compared to responsive design. This is mainly because in responsive design, you need to do a complete overhaul of the site design, whereas in adaptive design, you just need to customize, optimize, and modify design styles to create an immersive end-user experience.

To infer, responsive web design is suitable for designing a new website, whereas adaptive design is favorable for retrofitting. Ultimately, it all boils down to user experience in this digital age - especially with the new generation preferring a *function-over-form* approach where the emphasis is more on ease of use and fruitful functionality than visual appeal. As we learned quite a bit about responsive design and adaptive design, moving forward, we will look at an overview of the potent UIkit framework in the next section.

Getting Started with UIkit

UIkit is an open source framework that helps you design sleek websites faster and easier. UIkit has baked-in cross-browser compatibility, default responsiveness, and handy CSS and JavaScript components, including proficient helper classes. You can build interactive, sophisticated designs; and in this book, we are going to show that in an organized step-by-step approach.

You can click on the following link to access the UIkit website:

- `https://getuikit.com`

Figure 1-1 shows the mobile UIkit website whereas Figure 1-2 shows the traditional desktop version.

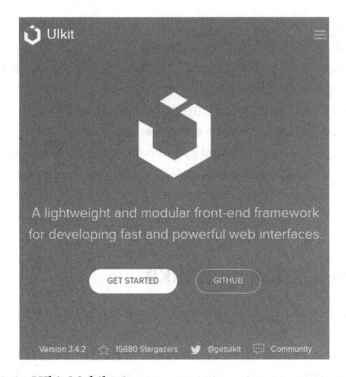

Figure 1-1. *UIkit Mobile site*

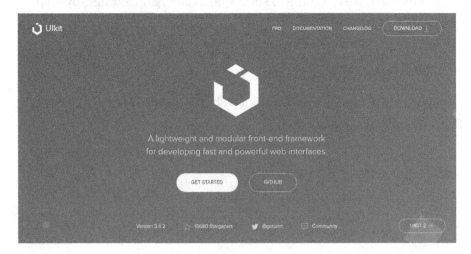

Figure 1-2. *UIkit Desktop website*

Both the preceding images clearly show the responsive nature of the UIkit website. For same/similar content, there is a difference in layout styles for the mobile and desktop platforms. As you can see, there is a hamburger icon on the mobile site, which on being clicked will show the different menu items defined as per the functionality for the mobile platform. In the next section, we will look at the different ways of installing UIkit.

Installing UIkit

There are many ways you can install UIkit for your web projects.

Method I

You can download the UIkit zip file by clicking on the DOWNLOAD button on the UIkit website. Figure 1-3 shows the **DOWNLOAD** button highlighted in a rectangular red box.

Figure 1-3. *Download button highlighted in red box*

Once you download the ZIP file, you have to unzip it. Figure 1-4 shows the content of the unzipped UIkit file.

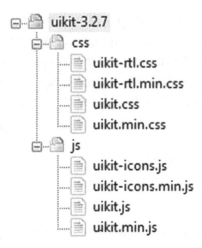

Figure 1-4. *Unzipped UIkit file structure*

You can define the path to the CSS and JS files in your HTML page for your web projects.

Method II

The easiest way to include UIkit and get going quickly is by using the CDN link for this framework. Listing 1-1 shows the specific markup to use the CDN link in your HTML file.

Listing 1-1. CDN links

```
<!--UIkit CSS -->
<link rel="stylesheet" href="https://cdn.jsdelivr.net/npm/
uikit@3.2.7/dist/css/uikit.min.css" />
<!--UIkit JS -->
<script src="https://cdn.jsdelivr.net/npm/uikit@3.2.7/dist/js/
uikit.min.js"></script>
<script src="https://cdn.jsdelivr.net/npm/uikit@3.2.7/dist/js/
uikit-icons.min.js"></script>
```

There are several advantages of using CDN links for your web projects. For starters, a CDN (read **Content Delivery Network**) holds copies of the file in several locations across multiple servers. The files can be images, fonts, scripts, and videos. The benefits include the following:

- *More servers*

- *Easy maintenance*

- *More bandwidth with high performance*

- *Redundancy for Fail-safe protection*

- *Optimized Caching settings*

- *Parallelized downloads*

Method III

You can use Yarn to get the pre-built JavaScript, CSS, and LESS source files.

Yarn is a popular JavaScript package manager that automates the process of installing, updating, configuring, and removing pieces of software (packages) retrieved from a global registry. LESS (which stands for Leaner Style Sheets) is a backward-compatible language extension for CSS.

The following commands have to be used for the process as shown in Listing 1-2.

Listing 1-2. Installing using Yarn

```
# Run once to install all dependencies
```

- **yarn add uikit**

    Alternatively, you can clone the GitHub repository to get all source files including build scripts.

- **git clone git://github.com/uikit/uikit.git**

  The GitHub project contains the source files in a compiled dist folder that contains a lot of additional files, which are not available by downloading the default Download link. If you use a custom UIkit theme, compiling will include other essential files too.

- `/src` - contains all JavaScript and image sources, including the Less files.

- `/dist` - contains all the compiled CSS and JS, which are incidentally updated on every release.

- `/tests` - contains HTML test files for all components.

  You can also compile UIkit yourself using the following build scripts, which are included in the GitHub files. The entire process is defined in the following link:

  `https://getuikit.com/docs/less`

  Initially, you need to run Yarn once to install all dependencies:

- **yarn install**

  To compile all source files, you need to use the following command:

- **yarn compile**

  To automate the compiling process each time a file changes or some updates are made, like modifying LESS files or updating the JavaScript code, you need to use the following command:

- **yarn watch**

Note   For the latest setup, you need to use Node.js version 8.2.0 or higher.

Remember, UIkit's core framework doesn't include some advanced components such as date pickers or Lightbox. So, if you are using UIkit's core framework, then you will find all the additional components in separate /css and /js folders.

Figure 1-5 shows the dist file structure, which includes the core UIkit framework and the css and js components folder along with their default files.

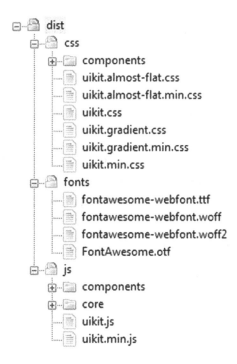

Figure 1-5. *File structure illustration of UIkit core framework with additional component folders*

The file structure contains the core and components folder; but by using it, you can include only those components that you will need to use in your website.

Summary

In this chapter, we saw an overview of the easy-to-use UIkit framework. We looked at the evolution of responsive web design. Next, we touched base with the basic ideologies of responsive and adaptive web design. Thereon, we looked at the different methods of installing UIkit in your web projects. In the next chapter, we will explain the Grid and Container layouts, ingrained FlexBox support characteristic, and utility helper classes that will help jumpstart your dive into the inner workings of this robust framework.

References

https://developer.mozilla.org/en-US/docs/Learn/CSS/CSS_layout/Responsive_Design

https://www.uxpin.com/studio/blog/responsive-vs-adaptive-design-whats-best-choice-designers/

https://learn.onemonth.com/responsive-vs-adaptive-vs-fluid-design/

CHAPTER 2

Grid System, Containers, and Helper Classes

UIkit enables you to create cross-platform websites with a simple code structure and minimalistic approach. You can create robust interfaces quickly using the array of components provided by this intuitive framework.

In this chapter, we will look at the Grid System, Containers, and Utility/ Helper elements that help build interactive designs, which account for a superior user experience.

Note In this book, we will be using Notepad++ as the editor for all the code examples. For the sample content, we will use the scoops from the http://www.catipsum.com website.

Rather than delving in too much theory, let's get started with this framework right away - by the end of this chapter, you will surely understand the grid and container concepts in addition to some helper classes, which will hold budding designers in good stead in their UIkit web projects.

© Aravind Shenoy 2020
A. Shenoy, *Jumpstart UIKit*, https://doi.org/10.1007/978-1-4842-6029-6_2

UIkit Starter Template

UIkit's starter template will be used as a base for all code examples in this book.

Listing 2-1 shows all the various links and supported scripts that are a part of the UIkitFramework.

Listing 2-1. Starter Template with CDN links

```
<!DOCTYPE html>
<html>
  <head>
  <meta charset="utf-8">
  <meta name="viewport" content="width=device-width, initial-
  scale=1">
  <title>Hello UIkit!</title>
    <!-- UIkit CSS -->
<link rel="stylesheet" href="https://cdn.jsdelivr.net/npm/
uikit@3.3.0/dist/css/uikit.min.css" />
<!-- UIkit JS -->
<script src="https://cdn.jsdelivr.net/npm/uikit@3.3.0/dist/js/
uikit.min.js"></script>
<script src="https://cdn.jsdelivr.net/npm/uikit@3.3.0/dist/js/
uikit-icons.min.js"></script>
  </head>
  <body style="padding: 50px 50px 50px 50px;">
    <div>
    <h1 class="title">
      Hello World
    </h1>
```

```
    <p class="subtitle">
      My first webpage with <strong>UIkit</strong>!
    </p>
  </div>

  </body>
</html>
```

In Listing 2-1, you can see the various links and styles in the <head> section. In the <head> section, the charset meta tag is used to define an HTML document's character set. The viewport meta tag helps web designers control the viewport (viewport is the portion of the web page visible to the users). While the width=device-width attribute sets the width of the page as per the device screen, initial-scale=1.0 instructs the device to display the page without any zooming.

Next, we define the following CDN link for incorporating UIkit's ingrained CSS styles:

```
<link rel="stylesheet" href="https://cdn.jsdelivr.net/npm/
uikit@3.3.0/dist/css/uikit.min.css" />
```

Moving forward, we define the following links for leveraging the functionality of JavaScript-related elements and icons baked into UIKit:

```
<script src="https://cdn.jsdelivr.net/npm/uikit@3.3.0/dist/js/
uikit.min.js"></script>
<script src="https://cdn.jsdelivr.net/npm/uikit@3.3.0/dist/js/
uikit-icons.min.js"></script>
```

Now that we are acquainted with the starter template, we will take a look at UIkit's Flexbox- Powered grid system.

Flexbox-Powered Grid Layout

There are several advantages of using a Grid layout such as good readability, page cohesiveness, and streamlined flexibility to name a few. (For in-depth information on CSS Grid layouts, you can refer to https://developer.mozilla.org/en-US/docs/Web/CSS/CSS_Grid_Layout.

UIkit is completely responsive by nature; and by default, all the grid cells are stacked. In UIkit, the grid attribute is used in conjunction with the Width component and Flex component to determine the length of each column and align/place/order items respectively.

Before understanding grids, let's understand how you split content into responsive cells in UIkit. For this we use the Width and the Grid components. We will look at how to use the width component and then use it in conjunction with the Grid component later on in the code samples.

Grids and Width

Width can be used in different ways, that is, using fractions, or auto-filling, or expansion utilities.

By using fractions, you can define the length of the columns spanning the 12-column grid. Following are the different fractions you can use for defining the length of the columns:

- uk-width-1-1 : - this fills out the entire width of the parent container

- uk-width-1-2 : - here, the width is equivalent to half of the parent container

- uk-width-1-3 :- here, the width is equivalent to one-third of the parent container

- uk-width-2-3 : - here, the width is equivalent to two-thirds of the parent container

- uk-width-1-4 : - here, the width is equivalent to one-fourth of the parent container

- uk-width-3-4 : - here, the width is equivalent to three-fourths of the parent container

- uk-width 1-5 : - here, the width is equivalent to one-fifth of the parent container

- uk-width 4-5 : - here, the width is equivalent to four-fifths of the parent container

- uk-width-1-6 : - here, the width is equivalent to one-sixth of the parent container

- uk-width-5-6 : - here, the width is equivalent to five-sixths of the parent container

The fractions have to be unique, and there is no redundancy while defining the length; for example, the fraction ²⁄₄ is the same as ½ - so we use uk-width-1-2 instead of using uk-width-2-4.

UIkit has a grid component that is usually used in conjunction with the width element. The grid module allows you to place the block elements in responsive columns. By default, all grid cells are stacked. Therefore, by defining the width of the column using the width component in tandem with the grid element, we can arrange the elements next to each other.

You can just add the uk-grid attribute to a <div> tag to create a grid container.

Note   Actually, there is also a **uk-grid** class you can add, but it is optional as it is automatically added using UIkit's JavaScript. Though in this book, we will just use the **uk-grid** attribute only - you may at times need to use **uk-grid** class in case the JavaScript gets deferred in real-time scenarios.

We will be using the card container elements in our examples to illustrate the functionality of how grid systems work. We will explain the card container code used in our examples - that way you can get a hang of this awesome utility, widely used in e-commerce and flat design-based modern layouts.

Let's look at a basic grid example shown in Listing 2-2.

Listing 2-2. Basic Grid Example

```
<div class="uk-text-center" uk-grid>
    <div class="uk-width-1-3">
        <div class="uk-card uk-card-default uk-card-body">
        Uno</div>
    </div>
    <div class="uk-width-2-3">
        <div class="uk-card uk-card-default uk-card-body">
        Dos</div>
    </div>
```

Listing 2-2 has a parent <div> tag to which we have assigned the **uk-grid** attribute in conjunction with the **uk-text-center** class. What this effectively does is position the content at the center of the elements, which are defined in that grid. Next, we create a child <div> element and assign the **uk-width-1-3** class, meaning the element will span a length of three equivalent columns for that grid. Within the child <div>, we create a sub-child and use the **uk-card**, **uk-card-default**, and **uk-card-body** classes to define the card element. The **uk-card** class will create a card component and **uk-card-body** class will create padding between the card and its corresponding content. Since a card in UIkit is blank by default, we assign the modifier **uk-card-default** class to define a styling for the card.

Moving forward, within the parent <div> element, we define another child <div> element and assign the **uk-width-2-3** class to it. Then we create another card with the same code as defined in the first card, except for the text content.

The output of the code is shown in Figure 2-1.

Figure 2-1. *Basic Grid with two card elements of different sizes*

If, for example, all the child elements are of equivalent size, then you can define the common width in conjunction with the **uk-grid** attribute itself. Following is Listing 2-3, where we have defined the width of the child containers in the parent container <div> element alongside the **uk-grid** attribute.

Listing 2-3. Assigning common width to all the child elements

```
<div class="uk-child-width-1-6 uk-text-center" uk-grid>
    <div>
        <div class="uk-card uk-card-default uk-card-body">
        Uno</div>
    </div>
    <div>
        <div class="uk-card uk-card-default uk-card-body">
        Dos</div>
    </div>
    <div>
        <div class="uk-card uk-card-default uk-card-
        body">Tres</div>
    </div>
        <div>
        <div class="uk-card uk-card-default uk-card-
        body">Cuatro</div>
    </div>
```

```
    <div>
    <div class="uk-card uk-card-default uk-card-
    body">Cinco</div>
 </div>
    <div>
    <div class="uk-card uk-card-default uk-card-
    body">Seis</div>
 </div>
</div>
```

In Listing 2-3, we create the parent <div> element and assign the **uk-child-width-1-6** class alongside the **uk-text-center** class and the **uk-grid** attribute. Then we define six child container <div> elements within the parent container and within those child containers, we create a card each using the same code as in Listing 2-2 for cards with default styling.

The **uk-child-width-1-6** class will result in each card spanning the length of 2 columns each in the 12-column default grid.

The output of the code is shown in Figure 2-2.

Figure 2-2. *Common width for all 6 cards*

You can define the auto and expand utilities in UIkit. While the auto-modifier will make the item span the width of its own content, the expand modifier will stretch and fill up the remaining space of the parent container.

You can also use the primary and secondary color modifier to style the elements. While the primary color modifier will result in the defined item gaining a blue color shade, the secondary color modifier will result in a shade of a black color.

Listing 2-4 shows an example of the color, auto, and expand modifiers.

Listing 2-4. Auto and Expand modifiers alongside contextual color modifiers

```
<div class="uk-text-center" uk-grid>
    <div class="uk-width-auto">
        <div class=" uk-card uk-card-body uk-card-primary">
        Cat ipsum dolor sit amet</div>
    </div>
    <div class="uk-width-expand">
        <div class="uk-card uk-card-body uk-card-secondary">
        Cat ipsum dolor sit amet</div>
    </div>
  </div>
```

In Listing 2-4, we define a parent <div> container and assign the centered text class and **uk-grid** attribute to it. Then we define two child elements, where we define a card for each child. The first child <div> container, which incorporates the first card, will have the **uk-width-auto** class assigned to it. Next, we define the primary color modifier to the first card using the **uk-card-primary** class assigned to it. What the **uk-width-auto** class does is enable the first element to span a width of its own content. The **uk-card-primary** class allocates a shade of a blue color to the card.

Coming back to the second child <div> container, we assign the **uk-width-expand** class. Thereon, we assign the **uk-card-secondary** class to the card within. The **uk-width-expand** class will enable the second element to span a width of the remaining space of that grid. The **uk-card-secondary** class will allocate a black shade to the card.

21

The output of the code is shown in Figure 2-3.

Figure 2-3. *Primary- and secondary-colored cards with auto and expand class implementation*

UIkit also has pre-defined widths, which can be used if you want those particular fixed widths for those elements. Remember, these are fixed widths for child containers, and Table 2-1 shows the metrics for the same.

Table 2-1. *Grid-Fixed Widths*

Fixed Width Classes	Metrics
uk-width-small	150px
uk-width-medium	300px
uk-width-large	450px
uk-width-xlarge	600px
uk-width-xxlarge	750px

Listing 2-5 shows an example of applying fixed widths.

Listing 2-5. Applying Fixed Widths

```
<div class="uk-text-center" uk-grid>
    <div class="uk-width-small">
        <div class="uk-card uk-card-default uk-card-body">
        Uno </div>
    </div>
```

```
<div class="uk-width-medium">
    <div class="uk-card uk-card-default uk-card-body
    uk-card-primary"> Dos </div>
</div>
<div class="uk-width-large">
    <div class="uk-card uk-card-default uk-card-body
    uk-card-secondary">Tres</div>
</div>
    <div class="uk-width-xlarge">
    <div class="uk-card uk-card-default uk-card-body
    uk-card-primary">cuatro</div>
</div>
    <div class="uk-width-xxlarge">
    <div class="uk-card uk-card-default uk-card-body
    uk-card-secondary">Cinco</div>
    </div>
</div>
```

In Listing 2-5, we create a grid within which we define five card elements. The child containers of the grid have been assigned the **uk-width-small**, **uk-width-medium**, **uk-width-large**, **uk-width-xlarge**, and **uk-width-xxlarge** classes, which will allocate a size equal to the metrics defined in Table 2-1.

Also, we have defined the default, primary, and secondary modifiers to the cards for achieving better clarity.

The output of the code is shown in Figure 2-4.

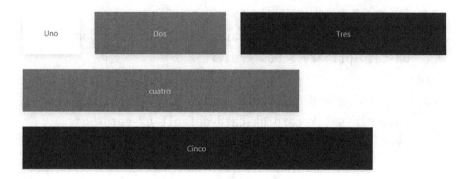

Figure 2-4. *Pre-defined Fixed widths implementation*

In UIkit, you can change the gap size for the grid by using the pre-defined different-sized grid padding classes. Listing 2-6 depicts an example for using ingrained, diverse gap modifiers.

Listing 2-6. Changing Gap sizes for grids

```
<div class="uk-grid-small uk-child-width-expand uk-text-center"
uk-grid>
    <div>
        <div class="uk-card uk-card-body uk-card-
        secondary">Uno</div>
    </div>
    <div>
        <div class="uk-card uk-card-body uk-card-primary">
        Dos</div>
    </div>
</div>
<br>
<div class="uk-grid-medium uk-child-width-expand uk-text-
center" uk-grid>
    <div>
```

```html
        <div class="uk-card uk-card-body uk-card-
        secondary">Uno</div>
    </div>
    <div>
        <div class="uk-card uk-card-body uk-card-primary">
        Dos</div>
    </div>
</div>
<br>
<div class="uk-grid-large uk-child-width-expand uk-text-center"
uk-grid>
    <div>
        <div class="uk-card uk-card-body uk-card-
        secondary">Uno</div>
    </div>
    <div>
        <div class="uk-card uk-card-body uk-card-primary">Dos
        </div>
    </div>
</div>
  <br>
<div class="uk-grid-collapse uk-child-width-expand uk-text-
center" uk-grid>
    <div>
        <div class="uk-card uk-card-body uk-card-
        secondary">Uno</div>
    </div>
    <div>
        <div class="uk-card uk-card-body uk-card-primary">
        Dos</div>
    </div>
</div>
```

In Listing 2-6, we create four grids. For the grid cells, we use the **uk-child-width-expand** and **uk-text-center** classes. The **uk-child-width-expand** class will ensure even space distribution for the items that are positioned in the same row. We define the **uk-grid-small**, **uk-grid-medium**, **uk-grid-large**, **uk-grid-collapse** for the four grids respectively. Thereon, for each grid, we define two cards of the secondary color and primary color respectively.

The output of the code can be seen in Figure 2-5.

Figure 2-5. *Different gap sizes defined for 4 grids*

In Figure 2-5, we can see increasing gaps between the items owing to the small, medium, and large gap classes assigned to each grid. In the fourth grid, we can see literally see no gap due to the collapse class assigned to the grid.

We can also assign individual gaps for each row and column in a grid. Listing 2-7 shows an illustration of the gap modifiers used for individual rows and columns.

Listing 2-7. Individual Row and Column Gap Modifiers

```
<div class="uk-grid-column-small uk-grid-row-small uk-child-
width-expand uk-text-center" uk-grid>
    <div>
        <div class="uk-card uk-card-body uk-card-
        secondary">Uno</div>
    </div>
    <div>
        <div class="uk-card uk-card-body uk-card-primary">
        Dos</div>
    </div>
</div>
<div class="uk-grid-column-large uk-grid-row-medium uk-child-
width-expand uk-text-center" uk-grid>
    <div>
        <div class="uk-card uk-card-body uk-card-
        secondary">Uno</div>
    </div>
    <div>
        <div class="uk-card uk-card-body uk-card-primary">
        Dos</div>
    </div>
</div>
<div class="uk-grid-column-collapse uk-grid-row-large uk-child-
width-expand uk-text-center" uk-grid>
    <div>
        <div class="uk-card uk-card-body uk-card-
        secondary">Uno</div>
    </div>
```

```
<div>
    <div class="uk-card uk-card-body uk-card-primary">
    Dos</div>
    </div>
</div>
```

In Listing 2-7, we use similar code as in Listing 2-6 except for the gap modifiers, where there are minor changes. We use the **uk-grid-column-small** and **uk-grid-row-small** classes as the gap modifiers for the first grid. For the second grid, we use the **uk-grid-column-large** and **uk-grid-row-medium** classes as the gap modifiers. For the third grid, we use the **uk-grid-column-collapse** and **uk-grid-row-large** classes as the gap modifiers.

That results in small row and column gaps for the first grid; medium and large gaps for the column and row in the second grid; and finally, collapsed column gaps and large gaps for the rows.

The output of the code is seen in Figure 2-6.

Figure 2-6. *Individual row and column gap modifiers*

UIkit also allows you to match the height of various cells in a grid, regardless of the content and padding of each cell; this resourceful aspect is quite handy in e-commerce sites where products with different descriptions and content are laid next to each other. In such cases, you can use the height match facility built into the UIkit framework.

Listing 2-8 shows an example where we match three grid cells with varying amounts of content.

Listing 2-8. Height Match utility

```
<div class="uk-grid-match uk-child-width-expand uk-text-center"
uk-grid>
    <div>
        <div class="uk-card uk-card-body uk-card-primary">Cat
        ipsum dolor sit amet, cupidatat officia tempor.Cat
        ipsum dolor sit amet, cupidatat officia tempor.</div>
    </div>
    <div>
        <div class="uk-card uk-card-body uk-card-primary">Cat
        ipsum dolor sit amet, cupidatat officia tempor.
        Cat ipsum dolor sit amet, cupidatat officia tempor.
        Cat ipsum dolor sit amet, cupidatat officia tempor.
        Cat ipsum dolor sit amet, cupidatat officia
        tempor.<br>...</div>
    </div>
    <div>
        <div class="uk-card uk-card-body uk-card-primary">Cat
        ipsum dolor sit amet, cupidatat officia tempor.
        Cat ipsum dolor sit amet, cupidatat officia tempor.
        Cat ipsum dolor sit amet, cupidatat officia tempor.
        Cat ipsum dolor sit amet, cupidatat officia tempor.
        Cat ipsum dolor sit amet, cupidatat officia tempor.
        Cat ipsum dolor sit amet, cupidatat officia
        tempor.<br>...<br>...</div>
    </div>
</div>
```

In Listing 2-8, the **uk-grid-match** class is used in tandem with the **uk-child-width-expand** and **uk-text-center** classes along with the **uk-grid** attribute. Then we define child <div> containers where we create three cards of primary contextual colors but with varying amount of content and line breaks (*think
*).

The output of the code is shown in Figure 2-7.

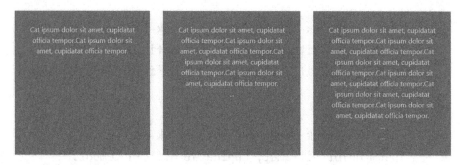

Figure 2-7. *Three grid cells of varying amount of content having equal height*

Next, we move on to the nested grid utility in UIkit. Listing 2-9 shows an excellent example of how grids are nested in UIkit.

Listing 2-9. Nested Grids

```
<div class="uk-child-width-1-2 uk-text-center" uk-grid>
    <div class="uk-padding" style="border: 7px solid Maroon;">
        <div class="uk-card uk-card-default uk-card-body uk-
        card-primary">UNO</div>
    </div>
    <div>
    <div class="uk-child-width-expand uk-text-center uk-
    padding" style="border: 7px solid Lime;" uk-grid>
            <div>
```

```
        <div class="uk-card uk-card-secondary uk-card-
        body">UNO</div>
    </div>
    <div>
        <div class="uk-card uk-card-secondary uk-card-
        body">UNO</div>
    </div>
    </div>
  </div>
</div>
```

In Listing 2-9, we create a parent <div> container and define the child width for that grid using the **uk-child-width-1-2** class, which will result in the child elements for that main grid spanning half the length of the 12-column default grid. Next, we move on to define the child <div> containers for that main grid.

For the first <div> child container, we use the **uk-padding** class to add padding for that element. We then use inline styles to define a *Maroon* border with *7px* thickness to that element. We define a card within and allocate a primary contextual color to it.

However, for the second <div> container, we define a nested grid by using the same **uk-grid** attribute along with the **uk-child-width-expand**, **uk-padding**, and **uk-text-center** classes. Thereon, we define a *Lime*-colored border of *7px* thickness using inline styles. Within this nested grid, we create two sub-child containers and define two primary contextual colored cards akin to many examples we have seen before.

The output of the code is shown in Figure 2-8.

Figure 2-8. *Nested grids*

UIkits have baked-in Flex properties that can be quite useful in modern layouts. Lots of UIkit's elements like Navbar, Tabs, and Pagination are created using Flexbox. By default, all the flex items display left alignment, take up as much width based on their content, and are of equal height as shown in Figure 2-9.

Note   We will just mention the sample content as "Cat Ipsum dolor sit …" in the book for illustration purposes and more clarity. The entire sample content in that code listing can be seen in the book's code bundle.

Listing 2-10. Flex feature

```
<div class="uk-flex">
    <div class="uk-card uk-card-body uk-background-muted">
    Cat ipsum dolor sit ...
    </div>
    <div class="uk-card uk-card-body uk-background-primary
    uk-light">Cat ipsum dolor sit ...
    </div>
    <div class="uk-card uk-card-body uk-background-secondary
    uk-light">Cat ipsum dolor sit amet   ...<div>
</div>
```

In Listing 2-10, we use the **uk-flex** class with the parent <div> container as we are using it as a block element (for an inline element, you need to use the *uk-flex-inline* class). Within this parent <div>, we create three child <div>s with the usual card container code. But instead of using uk-card-default styling, we have applied contextual colored backgrounds to the three cards using the **uk-background-muted**,

uk-background-primary, and **uk-background-secondary** classes. We have also used **uk-light** class to the primary-colored card and secondary-colored card for better visibility.

The output of the flex-powered code is shown in Figure 2-9.

Figure 2-9. Flex Items displaying equal height and content-relevant width

In Figure 2-9, you can see the Flex items next to each other without any gaps or padding - meaning flex items are laid next to each other without any gaps, margins, or padding.

You can also observe the background contextual colors applied to the three cards - and yes, despite varying content, all the three cards are of equal height due to the default Flex behavior in UIkit.

The Flex feature helps you immensely in alignment, especially when you are building intricate websites. Let's look at an example in Listing 2-11 where we align the flex items to the right.

Listing 2-11. Flex-powered right-side alignment

```
<div class="uk-flex uk-flex-right">
    <div class="uk-card uk-card-body uk-background-muted">Cat
    ipsum dolor </div>
    <div class="uk-card uk-card-body uk-margin-left uk-
    background-primary uk-light">Cat ipsum dolor </div>
    <div class="uk-card uk-card-body uk-margin-left uk-
    background-secondary uk-light">Cat ipsum dolor</div>
    </div>
```

Listing 2-11 shows the **uk-flex** and **uk-flex-right** classes assigned to the parent <div> container. Then we create three card child containers. For the first card, we use the muted contextual color for the background.

In the second and third cards, we use primary and contextual colors with the **uk-light** class for better visibility. We also use the **uk-margin-left** class for these two cards. The margin helps induce a gap between the cards (remember that in Flex aspects of UIkit, the items are laid next to each other without any gaps or padding).

The output of the code is shown in Figure 2-10.

***Figure 2-10.** Flex items with right alignment*

UIkit enables you to define vertical alignment of flex items. Listing 2-12 shows an example where we have centered the flex items along the cross axis using the **uk-flex-middle** class. In the same example, we have centered the items at the center of the web page using the **uk-flex-center** class.

***Listing 2-12.** Middle alignment of Flex items across the cross axis*

```
<div class="uk-flex uk-flex-middle uk-flex-center">
    <div class="uk-card uk-card-body uk-margin-left uk-
    background-primary uk-light">Cat ipsum dolor </div>
    <div class="uk-card uk-card-body uk-margin-left uk-
    background-primary uk-light">Cat ipsum dolor <br>Cat ipsum
    dolor<br>Cat ipsum dolor</div>
    <div class="uk-card uk-card-body uk-margin-left uk-
    background-primary uk-light">Cat ipsum dolor<br>Cat ipsum
    dolor<br>Cat ipsum dolor<br>Cat ipsum dolor<br>Cat ipsum
    dolor</div>
    </div>
```

Listing 2-12 includes a <div> container and the **uk-flex**, **uk-flex-middle**, and **uk-flex-center** classes that are assigned to it. Then we create three cards with the primary contextual color for the card background. We have increased the amount for the second and third cards using line breaks. Flex items are laid next to each other without any gaps or padding - that's why we use the **uk-margin-left** classes for the second and third flex items as we need to induce equivalent space between the cards.

The output of the code is shown in Figure 2-11.

Figure 2-11. *Flex items aligned across the middle cross axis and centered on the page*

You can also create vertical columns using the Flex property. Listing 2-13 shows an illustration of the vertical column alignment in UIkit.

Listing 2-13. Vertical Columns

```
<div class="uk-flex uk-flex-column uk-child-width-1-6 uk-text-center">
<div class="uk-card uk-card-body  uk-margin-bottom
uk-background-secondary uk-light">UNO </div>
<div class="uk-card uk-card-body  uk-margin-bottom
uk-background-primary uk-light">DOS </div>
<div class="uk-card uk-card-body  uk-margin-bottom
uk-background-secondary uk-light">TRES </div>
</div>
```

In Listing 2-13, we use the **uk-flex-column**, **uk-flex**, and **uk-child-width-1-6** and **uk-text-center** classes with the parent <div> container. The **uk-flex-column** class will result in vertical alignment of the flex items, and therefore, you can observe vertical columns. The width child class will allocate one-sixth of the length for each child container alongside the text center class, which will center the text in the card element. Like in the previous examples, we allocate secondary and primary contextual colors to the cards and use the **uk-margin-bottom** class in conjunction to induce space between the three flex items.

The output of the code is shown in Figure 2-12.

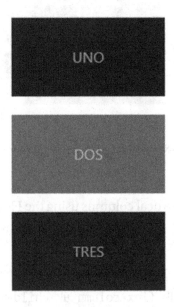

Figure 2-12. *Vertical Alignment of Flex Items*

By default, UIkit's flex items are positioned within one line. However, you can use the wrap flex property that will enable the items to occupy the next row if they don't fit into the same row. You can also reverse the sequence of the order in the wrap property. In addition, you can allocate the space equally at the top and bottom of each row. Let's see a code example in Listing 2-14, which depicts the same.

Listing 2-14. Wrap and Wrap-around utility

```
<div class="uk-flex uk-flex-wrap uk-flex-wrap-around">
            <div class="uk-width-1-2 uk-margin-right
            uk-margin-medium-bottom uk-card uk-card-body
            uk-card-primary">Uno</div>
            <div class="uk-width-1-3 uk-margin-right
            uk-margin-medium-bottom uk-card uk-card-body
            uk-card-primary">Dos</div>
            <div class="uk-width-1-2 uk-margin-right
            uk-margin-medium-bottom uk-card uk-card-body
            uk-card-primary">Tres</div>
            <div class="uk-width-1-4 uk-margin-right
            uk-margin-medium-bottom uk-card uk-card-body
            uk-card-primary">Cuatro</div>
</div>
```

In Listing 2-14, we have used the **uk-flex-wrap** and **uk-flex-wrap-around** classes for the parent <div> container. Then we created four child card containers of different sizes and assigned the primary contextual colors to it.

Next, we define the margins for right and bottom. What the **uk-flex-wrap** class does is fit the items in the second row if they exceed the length of the first row. Thereon, we use the **uk-flex-wrap-around** classes, which helps create equal space between the top and bottom rows.

The output of the code is shown in Figure 2-13.

Figure 2-13. *Flex Items Wrap feature*

In Figure 2-13, the first two flex items occupy the first row followed by the next two items occupying the second row as they exceeded the width of the 12-column grid of the parent container.

To change the item direction from right to left, you can use the **uk-flex-wrap-reverse** class instead as shown in Listing 2-15.

Listing 2-15. Wrap reverse utility

```
<div class="uk-flex uk-flex-wrap-around uk-flex-wrap-reverse">
        <div class="uk-width-1-2 uk-margin-right uk-margin-
        medium-top uk-card uk-card-body uk-card-primary">
        Uno</div>
    <div class="uk-width-1-3 uk-margin-right uk-margin-medium-
    top uk-card uk-card-body uk-card-primary">Dos</div>
        <div class="uk-width-1-2 uk-margin-right uk-
        margin-medium-top uk-card uk-card-body uk-card-
        primary">Tres</div>
        <div class="uk-width-1-4 uk-margin-right uk-
        margin-medium-top uk-card uk-card-body uk-card-
        primary">Cuatro</div>
</div>
```

The uk-flex-wrap-reverse class will change the direction of the items from right to left. The rest of the code is the same as the previous listing.

The output of the code is shown in Figure 2-14.

Figure 2-14. *Wrap reverse property*

In UIkit, the flex items are placed based on the source code. But you can use the flex first and last classes to change the order. Let's look a code example in Listing 2-16 to understand this.

Listing 2-16. First and Last Item repositioning

```
<div class="uk-flex">
      <div class="uk-card uk-card-default uk-card-body
      uk-background-muted uk-margin-left">
            Lorem ipsum dolor sit amet, consectetur
            adipisicing
      </div>
      <div class="uk-card uk-card-primary uk-card-body
      uk-margin-left uk-flex-last ">
      Lorem ipsum dolor sit amet, consectetur adipisicing
      </div>
      <div class="uk-card uk-card-secondary uk-card-body
      uk-margin-left uk-flex-first ">
      Lorem ipsum dolor sit amet, consectetur adipisicing
      </div>
   </div>
```

In Listing 2-16, we have used the flex property for the parent <div> element, within which we have defined the code for three cards, one with background muted, the second with a primary contextual color, and third with a secondary contextual color. For the second card, we have assigned the **uk-flex-last** class and for the third card, we have assigned the **uk-flex-first** class.

As a result, the second card will be placed last and the third card would be placed first on executing the code. We have also set margins for each card to allocate some space between the cards.

The output of the code is shown in Figure 2-15.

Figure 2-15. *Flex Items order sequence arranged*

Suppose you do not want any containers and you just want the content to be displayed in multiple columns: then you can use the column class facility as shown in Listing 2-17.

Listing 2-17. Content placed without containers in columns

```
<div class="uk-column-1-3">
    <p>Cat ipsum dolor sit amet, cupidatat ...</p>
    <p>Cat ipsum dolor sit amet, cupidatat... </p>
    <p>Cat ipsum dolor sit amet, cupidatat ...</p>
</div>
```

(*Note that in Listing 2-17, just like others, we have just denoted the sample content in only three words - the entire sample content can be seen in the code bundle.*)

The output of the code is shown in Figure 2-16

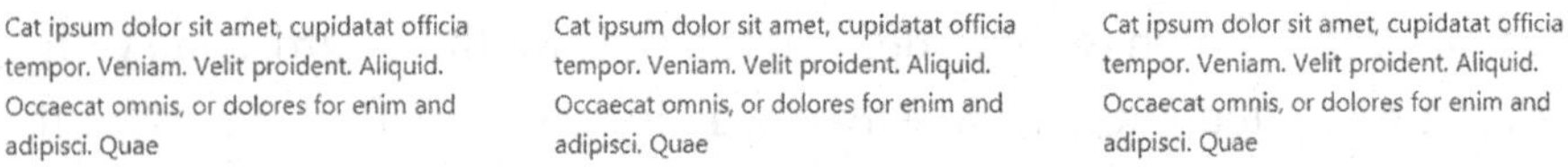

Cat ipsum dolor sit amet, cupidatat officia tempor. Veniam. Velit proident. Aliquid. Occaecat omnis, or dolores for enim and adipisci. Quae

Cat ipsum dolor sit amet, cupidatat officia tempor. Veniam. Velit proident. Aliquid. Occaecat omnis, or dolores for enim and adipisci. Quae

Cat ipsum dolor sit amet, cupidatat officia tempor. Veniam. Velit proident. Aliquid. Occaecat omnis, or dolores for enim and adipisci. Quae

Figure 2-16. *Content spread over different columns without containers*

Containers

In today's web design projects, you just don't add text and graphics in an ad hoc way. Here is where the concept of containers comes in. Using the container facility, you can group text, headings, buttons, media, and icons in a single group. Therefore, you can resize, move, adjust, alter, and place the entire container group instead of moving single objects.

UIkit provides the section and container classes with ultimate flexibility, which are effective controls in modern layouts. Usually, the container class is used in tandem with the section class in UIkit as shown in Listing 2-18.

Listing 2-18. Section and Container utility

```
<div class="uk-section uk-section-primary uk-light">
    <div class="uk-container">
        <div class="uk-grid-match uk-child-width-1-3 uk-text-
        center" uk-grid>
            <div>
                <p>Uno</p>
            </div>
            <div>
                <p>Duo</p>
            </div>
            <div>
                <p>Tres</p>
            </div>
        </div>
    </div>
</div>
```

In Listing 2-18, we have used the **uk-section** class along with the **uk-section-primary** and **uk-light** classes for enabling a primary-colored section with better visibility. Then we create a child <div> under the parent <div> and assign the **uk-container** class to it. Next we create a grid inside that container and use the height match attribute for all the three child elements within the grid.

The output of the code is shown in Figure 2-17.

Figure 2-17. *Code for Section and the inclusive container component*

You can add different paddings to both the container as well as the sections as shown in Listing 2-18. We proceed with the same code in Listing 2-17 and then add two more sections with the same structure, except for two changes in the code. For the second section, we add just the **uk-section-xsmall** class to the parent container <div> for the second section.

For the third section, we add the **uk-section-xsmall** class to the third section and add the **uk-container-xsmall** class to the child <div> container within the third parent <div> section container.

The entire code is shown in Listing 2-19.

Listing 2-19. Container and Sections with different-size allocation

```
<div class="uk-section uk-section-primary uk-light">
    <div class="uk-container">
        <div class="uk-grid-match uk-child-width-1-3 uk-text-
        center" uk-grid>
            <div>
```

```
                <p>Uno</p>
            </div>
            <div>
                <p>Duo</p>
            </div>
            <div>
                <p>Tres</p>
            </div>
        </div>
    </div>
</div>
<br><br>
<div class="uk-section uk-section-primary uk-section-xsmall uk-
light">
    <div class="uk-container">
        <div class="uk-grid-match uk-child-width-1-3 uk-text-
        center" uk-grid>
            <div>
                <p>Uno</p>
            </div>
            <div>
                <p>Dos</p>
            </div>
            <div>
                <p>Tres</p>
            </div>
        </div>
    </div>
</div>
<br><br>
```

```
<div class="uk-section uk-section-primary uk-section-xsmall uk-
light">
    <div class="uk-container uk-container-xsmall">
        <div class="uk-grid-match uk-child-width-1-3 uk-text-
        center" uk-grid>
            <div>
                <p>Uno</p>
            </div>
            <div>
                <p>Dos</p>
            </div>
            <div>
                <p>Tres</p>
            </div>
        </div>
    </div>
</div>
```

The output of the code is shown in Figure 2-18.

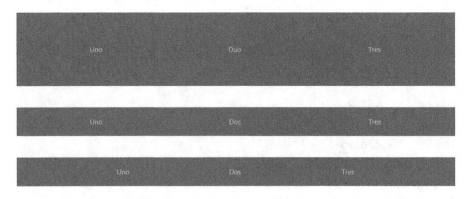

Figure 2-18. *Different Section and Container-sized elements*

In Figure 2-18, the second section is smaller because of the smaller-size class assigned to the section. Whereas the third section shows the text shifting inward because of the smaller size assigned to the third section with an ultra-smaller size assigned to the container element of the smaller section.

Utility Classes

Utility classes are useful helpers that define the styling of elements in the markup without using CSS style sheets. As they are directly used in the markup, they aid in quick development. Apart from ease of use, these modules can be used multiple times, adhering to the DRY principle. They also equip you with a high degree of consistency in your web projects.

Floats

UIkit provides the float utility in which you can place the items at the left or right of the container. UIkit also provides the Clearfix facility to prevent the element from overflowing outside the container if the element is taller than its container.

Listing 2-20. Float and Clearfix

```
<div class="uk-clearfix">
    <div class="uk-float-left">
        <div class="uk-card uk-card-primary uk-card-body">
        UNO </div>
    </div>
        <div class="uk-float-right">
        <div class="uk-card uk-card-secondary uk-card-
        body">DOS</div>
    </div>
</div>
```

In Listing 2-20, we assign the **uk-clearfix** class to the parent container. Then we create two child <div> elements with the parent <div>. To the first child <div>, we assign the **uk-float-left** class and define a primary contextual colored card within it. For the second child <div>, we assign the **uk-float-right** class and define a secondary contextual colored card within it.

Therefore, the first card will be positioned to the left of the page whereas the second card will be placed at the right of the page.

The output of the code is shown in Figure 2-19.

Figure 2-19. *Float classes with Clearfix*

Border Radius

UIkit has three classes for modifying the border radius of an element, namely – **uk-border-rounded**, **uk-border-circle**, and **uk-border-pill**. Let's check out an example in Listing 2-21.

Listing 2-21. Rounded Image Corners, Circular Images, and Pill-shaped images

```
<img class="uk-border-rounded" src="Images/Mick.png"
width="150" height="150" alt="Border rounded">
        <br><br>
<img class="uk-border-circle" src="Images/Oracle.png"
width="150" height="150" alt="Border circle">
        <br><br>
<img class="uk-border-pill" src="Images/Shrek.png" width="150"
height="150" alt="Border pill">
```

Now we have applied the three border classes to the three image elements, that is, uk-border-rounded class, uk-border-circle, and uk-border-pill.

The output of the code is shown in Figure 2-20.

Figure 2-20. *Rounded corners, Rounded Circle, and Pill Images*

In Figure 2-20, the first image has rounded corners, second has a circular shape, and third image has a pill shape as defined in the code.

Box Shadow

You can also apply box shadows to elements in UIkit. UIkit allows you to apply box shadows of different types, namely – small, medium, large, and extra-large. Listing 2-22 is an apt illustration to understand this.

Listing 2-22. Box Shadow

```
<div class="uk-flex uk-flex-center">
        <img class="uk-border-pill uk-box-shadow-medium"
        src="Images/Mick.png" width="150" height="150"
        alt="Mickey">
        </div>
        <br><br><br>
    <div class="uk-text-center" uk-grid>
     <div class="uk-width-1-2">
        <div class="uk-card uk-card-primary uk-card-body
        uk-box-shadow-large">SHREK</div>
     </div>

        <div class="uk-width-1-3">
        <div class="uk-card uk-card-secondary uk-card-body
        uk-box-shadow-xlarge">FIONA</div>
     </div>
  </div>
```

First we create a parent <div> element and use the **uk-flex** and **uk-flex-center** to position the child of the parent <div> to the center. Then we include an image and apply the **uk-border-pill** to generate a pill-shaped image. Then we add the line breaks.

Next, we create another parent <div> and assign the **uk-grid** attribute to it. Then within the grid, we create two child <div> elements and assign a width of 1/2 to the first <div>, enclosing a primary-colored card. We assign the large box shadow to this card using the **uk-box-shadow-large** shade to it.

For the second <div> child element, we assign a width of 1/3rd and define a secondary-colored card and assign the **uk-box-shadow-xlarge** class to it.

As a result, the first image will have a medium-sized shadow. The first card after the line break will have a large shadow while the second card next to it will have an extra-large box shadow.

In Figure 2-21, you can see a shadow below the three elements as defined in the code.

Figure 2-21. *Box shadows applied to the image and cards*

You can also add a box shadow on hovering over the element, meaning only when you hover on that element, a box shadow can be seen as shown in Listing 2-23.

Listing 2-23. Box shadow on Hover

```
<div class="uk-width-1-3">
    <div class="uk-card uk-card-secondary uk-card-body
    uk-box-shadow-hover-xlarge">FIONA</div>
    </div>
</div>
```

In Listing 2-23, we create just a secondary-colored card and applied the **uk-box-shadow-hover-xlarge** class to it. On executing the code, we see a secondary-colored card and when you hover, you can observe a extra-large box shadow around it. The output of the code on hovering over the secondary-colored card is shown in Figure 2-22.

Figure 2-22. *Box shadow on card after hovering over it*

Drop Cap

The drop cap feature in UIkit helps you to enlarge the first letter of the word, thereby indicating that it is the beginning of the text or paragraph. It delivers emphasized visual cues, usually seen in print designs - a code example is depicted in Listing 2-24.

Listing 2-24. Drop Cap feature

```
<div>
 <p class="uk-dropcap">World Wide Web (WWW), commonly known as
  the Web, is an information system where documents and other web
  resources are identified by Uniform Resource Locators (URLs,
  such as https://www.example.com/), which may be interlinked ....</p>
</div>
```

What we have done is assign the **uk-dropcap** class to the paragraph element. The resulting output will have the first letter in a Drop Cap visual cue as shown in Figure 2-23.

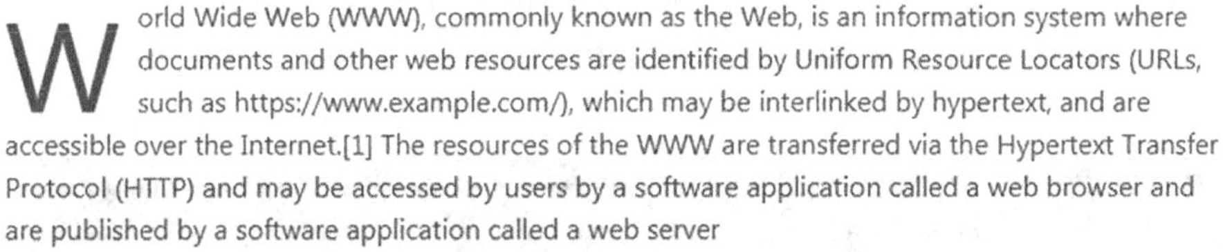

W orld Wide Web (WWW), commonly known as the Web, is an information system where documents and other web resources are identified by Uniform Resource Locators (URLs, such as https://www.example.com/), which may be interlinked by hypertext, and are accessible over the Internet.[1] The resources of the WWW are transferred via the Hypertext Transfer Protocol (HTTP) and may be accessed by users by a software application called a web browser and are published by a software application called a web server

Figure 2-23. Drop Cap feature

Logo

UIkit also enables you to create a logo for your site needs as shown in Listing 2-25 where we will create two logos, a text-based one and the other an image-based one.

Listing 2-25. Text and Image logos

```
<div class="uk-panel uk-padding uk-background-secondary uk-light">
    <a class="uk-logo" style="color: Gold;" href="https://www.
    apress.com/in"><b>Apress</b></a>
</div>
```

```
<br><br><br>
<div class="uk-panel uk-padding uk-background-secondary uk-light">
    <a class="uk-logo" href="https://www.apress.com/in"><img
    src="Images/Apress.png" alt="Apress"></a>
</div>
```

In Listing 2-25, we have created two panels using the **uk-panel** class by assigning it to two <div> elements.

Within the first <div> element, we have used the **uk-logo** class and assigned the Gold colored style for the *Apress* text in the content for that <div>.

For the second <div> element, we have used the **uk-logo** class and defined an image and entered the *Apress* Image in PNG format.

The output of the code is shown in Figure 2-24.

Figure 2-24. *Text and Image Logo*

In Figure 2-24, you can see the Apress text logo in the first panel and the Apress Image logo in the panel below it.

Summary

In this chapter, we looked at the Grid System and its concepts, Container utility, and a bunch of helper classes. There are a plethora of attributes than those mentioned, and you can find out about more utility classes at `https://getuikit.com/docs/utility`. Now that we have an idea about how grids and containers work, in the next chapter, we will move forward to understanding the intuitive Navigation elements and Media attributes.

CHAPTER 3

Navigation Elements and Media Attributes

This chapter examines UIkit's navigational elements and media attributes. UIkit's intuitive navigational elements enable access to content and commercial functionality such as checkout areas. The media attributes enable sophisticated web design. Let's look at the navigational elements first, followed by the media attributes.

Navigation

Website users should be able to find content easily and quickly. Therefore, streamlining navigation is critical for usability purposes and defines effectual web design. UIkit's navigation elements organize content effectively, and in this section, we are going to define the following components:

- Dropdown

- List Navigation

- Tabs

- Navbar

Dropdown

In UIkit, we can define a dropdown by using the **uk-dropdown** attribute on a block element. You can use a button or any content to toggle a dropdown. To group the toggle and dropdown, you need to add the **uk-inline** class to the container element that houses the block element and the content that toggles the dropdown. By default, you need to hover to see the dropdown. But you can add the **mode: click** property to the **uk-dropdown** attribute to enable the click functionality.

Let's look at an example in Listing 3-1 to see both the hover and click functionality.

Listing 3-1. Hover and Click Dropdown

```
<div class="uk-inline">
    <button class="uk-button uk-button-default">Hover
    Function</button>
    <div uk-dropdown>Cat ipsum dolor sit amet, cougar for american
    shorthair. Devonshire rex thai birman singapura</div>
</div>

<div class="uk-inline">
    <button class="uk-button uk-button-default">Click
    Function</button>
    <div uk-dropdown="mode: click">Havana brown norwegian
    forest, for tom jaguar. Abyssinian havana brown. Grimalkin
    himalayan</div>
</div>
```

In Listing 3-1, we define a parent container <div> element and assign the **uk-inline** class to it. Within it, we include a <button> element and assign the **uk-button** and **uk-button-default** classes to it. Thereon, we assign a <div> element to which we assign the **uk-dropdown** attribute to toggle the dropdown content.

Similarly, we create another parent <div> container and use similar code and different sample content. The only major difference here is that we assign the **mode: click** property to the **uk-dropdown** attribute to enable click functionality.

When we hover over the first button, the content is displayed in the dropdown. When we click on the second button, the content is displayed in the dropdown. We have grouped the two screenshots, one for the hover function and the other for the click function, in Figure 3-1 (in the image below, we have bordered the two boxes in red for illustration purposes).

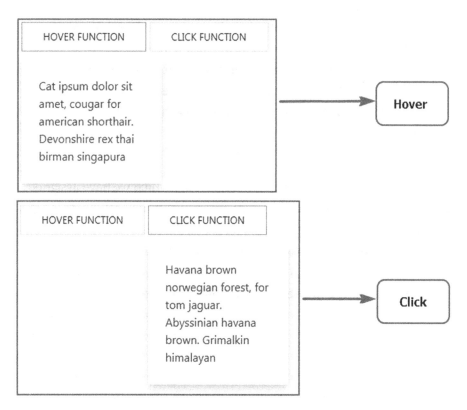

Figure 3-1. *Hover and Click Functionality*

UIkit provides different options to adjust the dropdown's alignment. You can see all the different dropdown positioning properties on the following page:

https://getuikit.com/docs/dropdown

In Listing 3-2, we will show the positioning, which is justified and aligned to the top.

Listing 3-2. Top-Justify alignment

```
<div class="uk-inline" style="padding: 250px 250px 250px
250px;">
    <button class="uk-button uk-button-default"> Hover Function
    </button>
    <div uk-dropdown="pos: top-justify">Cat ipsum dolor sit
    amet, cougar for american shorthair. Devonshire rex thai
    birman singapura maine cougar. Munchkin mink bobcat. Civet
    lynx </div>
</div>
```

We have used the container <div> element to which we have assigned the **uk-inline** class. Then we have defined a Hover button following which we have defined the dropdown content. For the child <div> for the dropdown toggle, we have assigned the **pos: top-justify** property to the **uk-dropdown** attribute.

The output of the code on hover is shown in Figure 3-2.

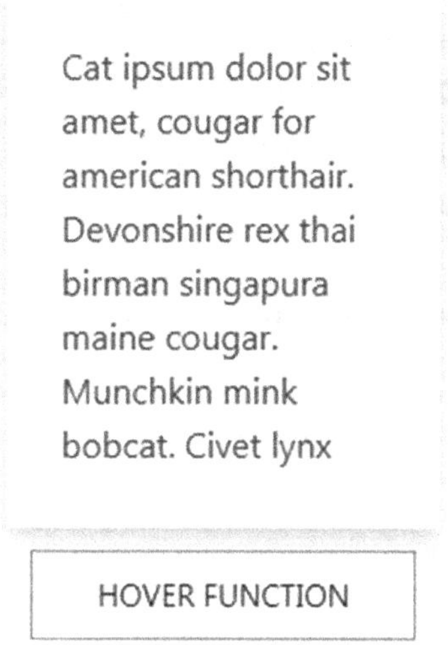

Cat ipsum dolor sit
amet, cougar for
american shorthair.
Devonshire rex thai
birman singapura
maine cougar.
Munchkin mink
bobcat. Civet lynx

HOVER FUNCTION

Figure 3-2. *Top-Justified alignment of the dropdown*

As you can see in Figure 3-2, on hovering, the dropdown is aligned to the top in a justified position context.

We can add animations to the dropdown element. For that, we will see an illustration in Listing 3-3.

Listing 3-3. Animation effect

```
<div class="uk-inline">
<button class="uk-button uk-button-default">Hover</button>
<div uk-dropdown="animation: uk-animation-shake; duration:
3000">
  <p>
  Cat ipsum dolor sit amet, cougar for american shorthair.
  Devonshire rex thai birman singapura maine cougar. Munchkin
  mink bobcat. Civet lynx
  </p>
</div>
</div>
```

In Listing 3-3, we have created a dropdown using the Hover functionality. However, we have assigned the **animation: `uk-animation-shake; duration: 3000`** property to the uk-dropdown attribute. The **`uk-animation-shake`** value will result in an animated shake effect to the left and right, and the **duration: 3000** value will define the effect to last for 3000 milliseconds.

The output of the code is shown in Figure 3-3.

HOVER

Cat ipsum dolor sit amet, cougar for american shorthair. Devonshire rex thai birman singapura maine cougar. Munchkin mink bobcat. Civet lynx

Figure 3-3. *Animation shake effect for 3000 ms*

In Figure 3-3, you can see the dropdown. Due to the animation effect, the dropdown will shake for a period of 3 seconds.

Let's look at List Navigations next.

List Navigations

List navigations are simple to use and save time. They provide a certain amount of consistency to the website and makes navigation hassle-free by organizing your content aptly. UIkit has diverse styles for list navigations. To activate the list navigation, you need to add the **uk-nav** class to the <ul> parent list element. By default the nav element has no styling - so you need to add the **uk-nav-default** class in conjunction with the **uk-nav** class as the modifier. To apply an active state to a menu item, you need to use the **uk-active** class in tandem.

Let's see an illustration in Listing 3-4.

Listing 3-4. List navigation

```
<div class="uk-width-1-2@s uk-width-2-5@m">
    <ul class="uk-nav uk-nav-default">
        <li class="uk-active"><a href="#">Home</a></li>
        <li><a href="#">Profile</a></li>
        <li><a href="#">Messages</a></li>
    </ul>
</div>
```

In Listing 3-4, we define a parent <div> class to which we assign the **uk-width-1-2@s** and **uk-width-2-5@m** classes to define the width on small screens and medium-and-above screens respectively. Then we define a list wherein we create a <ul> element and assign the **uk-nav** and **uk-nav-default** classes to it. Next we create the list items using the <li> elements. For the first list item, we assign the **uk-active** class and then create an anchor <a> tag within for the nav item.

Similarly, we define the other list items without the active class. The output of the code is shown in Figure 3-4.

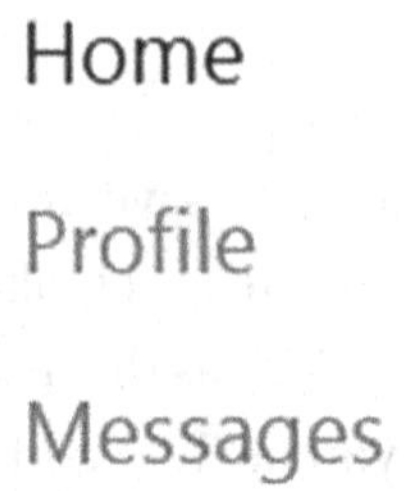

Home

Profile

Messages

Figure 3-4. *List Navigations*

Figure 3-4 shows the list navigation items, Home, Profile, and Messages where the Home Item is in an active state.

You can define a distinctive style for the list navigations using the **uk-nav-primary** class in conjunction with the **uk-nav** class. We use the same code as in Listing 3-4, but here we use the **uk-nav-primary** class in conjunction with the **uk-nav** class instead of the default class (refer to Listing 3-5).

Listing 3-5. Primary Modifier List navigation

```
<div class="uk-width-1-2@s uk-width-2-5@m">
    <ul class="uk-nav uk-nav-primary">
        <li class="uk-active"><a href="#">Home</a></li>
        <li><a href="#">Profile</a></li>

        <li><a href="#">Messages</a></li>
    </ul>
</div>
```

In Listing 3-5, we use the same code as in Listing 3-4 but we use the **uk-nav-primary** class in conjunction with the **uk-nav** class. The output of the code is shown in Figure 3-5.

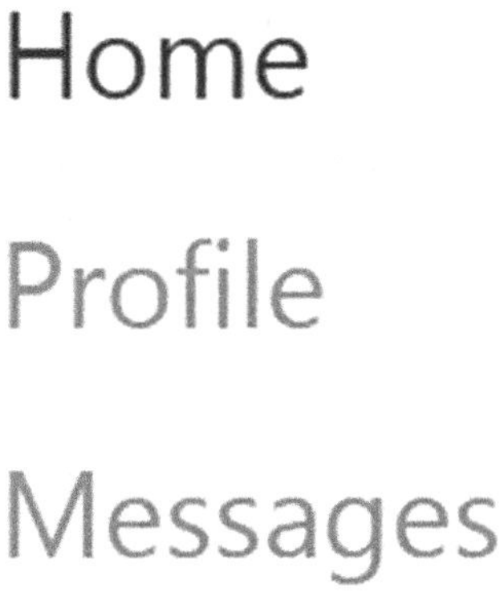

Home

Profile

Messages

Figure 3-5. *List navigations with Primary Modifier*

You can see the distinct effect in the way the list items are displayed in Figure 3-5.

You can introduce a divider between the list items using the **uk-nav-divider** class as shown in Listing 3-6.

Listing 3-6. List Navigations with divider

```
<div class="uk-width-1-2@s uk-width-2-5@m">
    <ul class="uk-nav uk-nav-primary">
        <li class="uk-active"><a href="#">Home</a></li>
        <li><a href="#">Profile</a></li>
            <li class="uk-nav-divider"> </li>
        <li><a href="#">Messages</a></li>
    </ul>
</div>
```

In Listing 3-6, we use the similar code as in Listing 3-5, but here we introduce a list item <li> between the 2nd and 3rd item and assign the **uk-nav-divider** class to it as highlighted in the code.

The output of the code is shown in Figure 3-6.

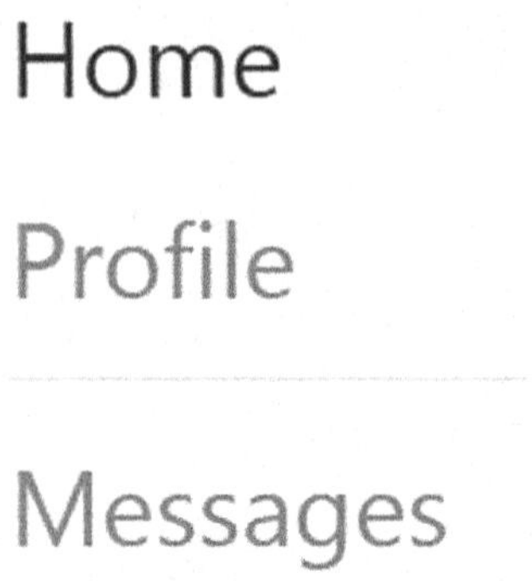

Home

Profile

Messages

Figure 3-6. *Dividers between List items*

You can clearly see a divider introduced between the 2nd and 3rd list item in Figure 3-6.

You can create nested navigation elements in UIkit. Let's look at an illustration in Listing 3-7.

Listing 3-7. Nested List Navigations

```
<div class="uk-width-1-2@s uk-width-2-5@m">
    <ul class="uk-nav uk-nav-primary">
        <li class="uk-active"><a href="#">Home</a></li>
        <li class="uk-parent">
            <a href="#">Messages</a>
            <ul class="uk-nav-sub">
                <li><a href="#">Inbox</a></li>
                <li><a href="#">Outbox</a></li>
        <li><a href="#">Sent</a></li>
        <li><a href="#">Spam</a></li>
            </ul>
        </li>
```

```
    <li><a href="#">Notifications</a></li>
  </ul>
</div>
```

In Listing 3-7, we create a parent <div> and assign the width classes to it. Then we create the main <ul> list tag and assign the **uk-nav** and **uk-nav-primary** classes to it. Thereon, we create the list items.

We define the first list item using the **uk-active** class with the <li> tag. Then we create the second list item. Here, we create a <li> tag and assign the **uk-parent** class to it. This will turn this item into a parent item. Then we define the item name within the <a> tags. Within this, we create a child <ul> element and assign the **uk-nav-sub** class to it. Within these child <ul> tags, we define the child list items using the <li> tags like we created before.

Finally, we create the last list item after the nested navigation list elements are created for the second list item. The output of the code is shown in Figure 3-7.

Home

Messages

Inbox

Outbox

Sent

Spam

Notifications

Figure 3-7. *Nested List Navigations*

In Figure 3-7, we can see that the second list item has four nested list items as defined in the code.

Let's look at Tab navigation next.

Tabs

UIkit has tabs-based navigation wherein clickable tabs are aligned next to each other. For tabs navigation, you need to use the **uk-tab** attribute.

Let's look at an illustration in Listing 3-8.

Listing 3-8. Tabs navigation

```
<ul uk-tab>
    <li class="uk-active"><a href="">Home</a></li>
    <li><a href="">Inbox</a></li>
    <li><a href="">Profile</a></li>
    <li><a href="">Notifications</a></li>
</ul>
```

In Listing 3-8, we have created an unordered list using the <ul> and <li> tags. To the <ul> element, we have assigned the **uk-tab** attribute. Within the <ul> tags, we have defined the <li> tags. For the first tab, we have used the **uk-active** class to make it the activated tab. Thereon, we have created the remaining list items for the other tabs.

The output of the code is shown in Figure 3-8.

HOME   INBOX   PROFILE   NOTIFICATIONS

Figure 3-8. *Tabbed Navigation*

You can see the tab navigation feature in Figure 3-8 where the first item is highlighted as defined in the code.

You can use the Flex component to align the tabs to the left or right. You can also flip tabs to the bottom using modifiers. Let's look at an illustration in Listing 3-9.

Listing 3-9. Flex alignment and Bottom Modifier

```
<div class="uk-margin-medium-top">
    <ul class="uk-flex-center" uk-tab>
        <li class="uk-active"><a href="#">Home</a></li>
        <li><a href="#">Profile</a></li>
        <li><a href="#">Notifications</a></li>
    </ul>
</div>
<br><br><br><br><br><br>
<div>
    <ul class="uk-flex-right" uk-tab>
        <li class="uk-active"><a href="#">Inbox</a></li>
        <li><a href="#">Outbox</a></li>
        <li><a href="#">Spam</a></li>
    </ul>
</div>
<br><br><br><br><br><br>
<div>
    <ul class="uk-tab-bottom" uk-tab>
        <li class="uk-active"><a href="#">About Us</a></li>
        <li><a href="#">Privacy Policy</a></li>
        <li><a href="#">Contact Us</a></li>
    </ul>
</div>
```

Initially, we create the first parent <div> container element within which we create an unordered list using the <ul> and <li> tags. For the <ul> element, we use the **uk-tab** attribute and assign the **uk-flex-center** class

67

to it, due to which tab items will be centered. Then, we define the list items just like in the previous tabs example.

For the next parent <div> container element, we create similar <ul> and <li> tags. But here, for the <ul> tag, we assign the **uk-flex-right** class in conjunction with the **uk-tab** attribute. This will align the tabs to the right of the container element. The rest of the code is similar to the previous <div> element, except for the name of the tabs.

Similarly, for the third <div> container element, we create similar <ul> and <li> tags. To the <ul> tag here, we assign the **uk-tab-bottom** class in tandem with the uk-tab attribute. This will flip the tabs to the bottom. The rest of the list items are defined similarly to the previous cases, except for the name of the tabs.

The output of the code is shown in Figure 3-9.

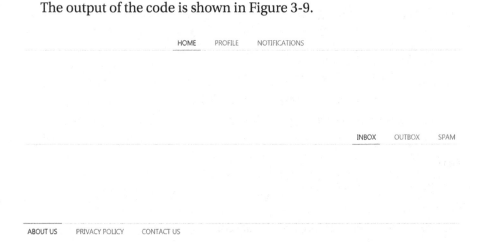

Figure 3-9. *Flex and Bottom Tab nav modifiers*

In Figure 3-9, you can see the first tab navigation centered whereas the second tab navigation is aligned to the right. The third tab navigation is flipped at the bottom.

We can introduce dropdowns in Tabbed navigation. Let's see an example of that in Listing 3-10.

Listing 3-10. Dropdown Tab Navigation

```
<ul uk-tab>
    <li class="uk-active"><a href="#">Home</a></li>
    <li><a href="#">Profile</a></li>
    <li>
        <a href="#">Messages <span class="uk-margin-small-left"
        uk-icon="icon: triangle-down"></span></a>
        <div uk-dropdown="mode: click">
            <ul class="uk-nav uk-dropdown-nav">
                <li class="uk-active"><a href="#">Inbox</a></li>
                <li><a href="#">Outbox</a></li>
                <li><a href="#">Spam</a></li>
                <li><a href="#">Trash</a></li>
            </ul>
        </div>
    </li>
    <li><a href="#">Notifications</a></li>
</ul>
```

Initially, in Listing 3-10, we create a parent <ul> element and assign the
uk-tab attribute to it. Then, we create three list items using the <li> tags.
For the first list item, we use the **uk-active** class to make it an activated tab.
Thereon, we create the second list item.

For the third list item, we will initially use the <li> tag, followed by
defining the tab item name within the anchor tags. Thereon, we introduce
a <span> element to create a dropdown triangle icon for that tab item. We
assign the **uk-icon** attribute to that <span> element and define the **icon:
triangle-down** value for creating a dropdown icon.

Next, we create a child <div> element within the third list item, to
which we assign the **uk-dropdown** attribute. We assign the **mode: click**
value to it to enable the click functionality that will display the dropdown.

Moving forward, we create a <ul> element within and assign the **uk-nav** and **uk-dropdown-nav** classes to it. This will create a list navigation and define the dropdown menu. Then we define the four list items for that list navigation, which will be displayed in the dropdown.

The output of the code will showcase the three tabs on the top. On clicking the third tab, the dropdown menu is displayed as shown in Figure 3-10.

Figure 3-10. *Dropdown menu in Tabbed navigation*

Figure 3-10 shows the dropdown menu as defined in the code.

In the next section, we will learn how to create a responsive Navbar element.

Navbar

A Navbar is an excellent way of organizing content. In UIkit, you can build a navigation bar with ease. However, for responsiveness, we will be using a bit of jQuery and CSS styles. Let's look at an example of a navigation bar in Listing 3-11.

Listing 3-11. Navbar Design

```
<header>
        <nav class="uk-navbar-container" uk-navbar>
           <div class="uk-navbar-left">
              <a href="index.html" class="uk-navbar-item
              uk-logo">
                 <img src="images/logo.jpg" class="logo"
                 alt="Apress Logo">
              </a>
              <a class="uk-navbar-toggle nav-none h123"
              id="nav_toggle">
                 <i uk-icon="icon: menu; ratio: 2"></i>

              </a>
              <div class="navbar-collapse" id="nav_
              collapse">
                 <ul class="uk-navbar-nav">
                    <li class="uk-active"><a
                    href=""><b>CATEGORIES</b></a></li>
                    <li class="uk-parent"><a
                    href=""><b>SERVICES</b></a></li>
                    <li class="uk-parent"><a
                    href=""><b>BLOG</b></a></li>
                    <li class="uk-parent"><a
                    href=""><b>WRITE</b></a></li>
                    <li><a href=""><b>SHOP</b></a></li>
                 </ul>
              </div>
           </div>
        </nav>
     </header>
```

In Listing 3-11, we have used an HTML <header> tag, which is a container for navigation links. Then we create a <nav> element and assign the **uk-navbar-container** class in conjunction with a **uk-navbar** attribute. The **uk-navbar** attribute defines the navbar component in UIkit. The **uk-navbar-container** class is used to define the navbar background style.

Thereon, we create a <div> element and assign the **uk-navbar-left** class to it. This will align the navigation of the items to the left of the navbar. Then we define the <a> tags within the <div> element and assign the **uk-navbar-item** class to it. Thereon, we introduce the image for the logo. This logo will be aligned to the left of the navbar as defined in the code.

Next, we create the hamburger icon. We create anchor <a> tags and use the **uk-navbar-toggle** class for the toggle functionality on mobile screens. Thereon, we assign the **nav-none** and **h123** classes to it along with **nav_toggle** as the id for the jQuery functionality and CSS styling. Then we define the menu icon and assign a ratio of 2 to it to increase the size of the hamburger icon twice the default icon size.

After that, we create the menu items. We create a <div> element and assign the **navbar-collapse** class and **nav_collapse** as the id for jQuery and CSS functionality.

Next, we create an unordered list using the <ul> element and assign the **uk-navbar-nav** class to it. This class will create the navigation, and then we define the menu items using the <li> element. We also use the **uk-active** class to indicate that the first menu item is an active one.

Note   We introduce the custom CSS stylesheet in the <head> section using the following link:

```
<link rel="stylesheet" href="style.css">
```

We also use the CDN link for jQuery and introduce the custom JavaScript file in the following <script> tags at the bottom of the html document before the closing <body> tag.

```
<script src="https://code.jquery.com/jquery-3.5.1.min.js"
integrity="sha256-9/aliU8dGd2tb6OSsuzixeV4y/faTqgFtohetphbbj0="
crossorigin="anonymous"></script>
```

```
<script src="navjs.js"></script>
```

Next we will explain the CSS code in Listing 3-12.

Listing 3-12. CSS style custom code

```
.nav-none{
    display: none;
}
#nav_toggle{
    position: absolute;
    right: 1em;
    top: 2em;
}
.h123{
    height: 35px;
    min-height: 35px;
}
.logo{ width: 100px; }

@media screen and (max-width:600px){
    .uk-navbar-left{
        display: block;
        width: 100%;
    }
    .uk-navbar-item{ display: inline; }

    .uk-navbar-nav{ display:block; }
    .navbar-collapse{ width:100%; }
    .uk-navbar-nav li{
```

```
      display: block;
      padding: 12px;
      height: 45px;
      border-bottom: 5px solid WhiteSmoke;
   }
   .uk-navbar-nav li a{
      display: block;
      width: 75%;
      padding: 1rem 1rem;
   }
}
```

Initially, we have used the **nav-none** class and set the display to none so that the hamburger icon is not seen on the large screen. Thereon, we have defined the position of the hamburger icon and defined the height. We set the width of the logo to 100px. From there, we have used a media query where the navbar will be displayed as a block element on a screen whose maximum width is equal or more than 600px.

We have defined the navbar width as 100% and then defined the padding and size, style, and color for the border.

Next, we will explain the JavaScript code in Listing 3-13.

Listing 3-13. Navjs jQuery file code

```
//media query event handler
// Sets Media query criteria to max-width of 600px and adds a
listener for keeping track of browser window size change.
// On line 7 this function has been called for setting media
query action based on the current browser width
if(matchMedia){
    const mq = window.matchMedia( "(max-width:600px)" );
    mq.addListener(WidthChange);
    WidthChange(mq)
```

```
}
// This function will be triggered everytime the browser is
resized
function WidthChange(mq){
    if(mq.matches){
        //if window width is less than or equal to 600px
        execute these lines of code
        $("#nav_toggle").removeClass("nav-none");  //makes
        toggler (burger icon) visible
        $("#nav_collapse").addClass("nav-none");//makes the
        normal expanded menu not visible
        //so you can only see the menu items when you click the
        toggler
        // Event handler added to the burger icon so that menu
        can be expanded and collapsed

        $("#nav_toggle").on('click', function(e){
            $("#nav_collapse").slideToggle(); // Slide the menu
            to full height containing the entire navigation if
            its hidden or vice versa
            $("#nav_collapse").css({"display": "block"}); //
            Set the visibility of the menu  to be visible
        })
    }else{
        //if window width is greater than 600px the else
        condition will be triggered
        $("#nav_toggle").addClass('nav-none'); // Hide the
        burger menu icon
        $("#nav_collapse").removeClass('nav-none'); //Show
        normal expanded navigation menu
    }
}
```

Initially, we set the media query criteria to a max width of 600px and add a listener for keeping track of changes in the browser window size. Later on, we call that function for setting media query action based on the current browser width.

After that, we set a function that will be triggered every time the browser is resized. The *if* condition specifies the condition that if the window width is less than or equal to 600px, it makes the hamburger icon visible (read *removeClass*). The next line (*addClass*) makes the normal expanded menu not visible in case the window width is less or equal to 600px. That way, you can only see the menu items when you click the hamburger icon. Then, an event handler is added to the hamburger icon so that the menu can be expanded and collapsed. This (read *slideToggle*) will slide the menu to full height containing the entire navigation if it is hidden or vice versa. The next line of code (*css*) will make the menu visible.

Then we use an *else* function wherein the following conditions will be triggered if the window width is greater than 600px. The following line (read *addClass*) will hide the hamburger menu icon in case of the window width being greater than 600px and the next line (read *removeClass*) will show the normal expanded navigation menu.

The output of the code on a desktop screen is shown in Figure 3-11.

Figure 3-11. *Navbar on a desktop screen*

On a smaller screen, the logo would be seen along with a hamburger menu icon. On clicking the icon, the menu items will be displayed as shown in Figure 3-12.

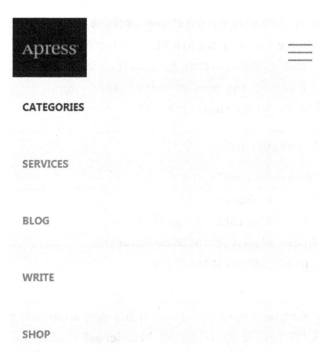

Figure 3-12. *Navbar with menu items on mobile screens*

As you can see, we have created a responsive navigation bar. Let's look at Breadcrumbs next.

Breadcrumbs

Breadcrumbs help direct users to the content flow and indicate the location on the website. They are quite handy when there are several nested webpages. They are often used in e-commerce websites as they reduce the actions needed to navigate to a higher-level page.

In UIkit, Breadcrumbs contain links that are aligned next to each other - a divider separates these links from each other. The last item in Breadcrumbs is highlighted as active by default in UIkit's Breadcrumbs.

All you need to do is assign the **uk-breadcrumb** class to the <ul> element and define the list items just like in other navigations. You usually use the <a> anchor element to define a link. If your list items do not need to be a link, in that case, you need to use the <span> tags.

Let's look at an example in Listing 3-14.

Listing 3-14. Breadcrumbs

```
<ul class="uk-breadcrumb">
    <li><a href="#">Home</a></li>
    <li><a href="#">Profile</a></li>
    <li><a href="#">Notifications</a></li>
    <li><span>Messages</span></li>
  </ul>
```

In Listing 3-14, we have created a list using the parent <ul> and child <li> elements. We have assigned the **uk-breadcrumb** class to the <ul> element. Thereon, we have defined three list items within the anchor tags and the last list item using the <span> tags within the <li> elements.

The output of the code is shown in Figure 3-13.

Home   /   Profile   /   Notifications   /   Messages

Figure 3-13. *Breadcrumbs utility*

In Figure 3-13, you can see that the first three list items are links whereas the last item is not a link as defined in the code. The last item is also highlighted though as per the default styling of Breadcrumbs in UIkit.

Let's look at Icon Navigation next.

Icon Navigation

You can create an icon navigation in UIkit easily. For that, you need to assign the **uk-iconnav** class to the <ul> list element. Let's look at an illustration in Listing 3-15.

Listing 3-15. Icon Navigation

```
<ul class="uk-iconnav">
    <li><a href="#" uk-icon="icon: home"></a></li>
    <li><a href="#" uk-icon="icon: settings"></a></li>
    <li><a href="#" uk-icon="icon: print"></a></li>
    <li><a href="#" uk-icon="icon: user"></a></li>
    <li><a href="#" uk-icon="icon: trash"></a></li>
  </ul>
```

In Listing 3-15, we have created a list using the parent <ul> and child <li> elements. We have assigned the **uk-iconnav** class to the <ul> element. Thereon, we created list items using the <li> elements and used anchor tags within to define the icons. We have used the **uk-icon** attribute and assigned the respective values to the icons to create different icons (*we will learn about icons in Chapter 4*).

The output of the code is shown in Figure 3-14.

Figure 3-14. *Icon Navigation*

Figure 3-14 displays the icon navigation where the icons are aligned side by side.

You can also align the list items in the icon navigation horizontally. For that, you need to use the **uk-iconnav-vertical** class in conjunction with the **uk-iconnav** class as shown in Listing 3-16.

Listing 3-16. Vertically-aligned Icon Navigation

```
<ul class="uk-iconnav uk-iconnav-vertical">
    <li><a href="#" uk-icon="icon: home"></a></li>
    <li><a href="#" uk-icon="icon: settings"></a></li>
    <li><a href="#" uk-icon="icon: print"></a></li>
        <li><a href="#" uk-icon="icon: user"></a></li>
    <li><a href="#" uk-icon="icon: trash"></a></li>
</ul>
```

In Listing 3-16, we have assigned the **uk-iconnav-vertical** class alongside the **uk-iconnav** class for the <ul> element. Thereon, we have defined the list items using the <li> elements and used the anchor tags for the icons similar to Listing 3-15.

The output of the code is shown in Figure 3-15.

Figure 3-15. *Vertically-aligned Icon Navigation*

Figure 3-15 shows vertically-aligned icon navigation as defined in the code.

Let's look at Sub Navigation next.

Sub Navigation

You can create a sub navigation in UIkit easily using the built-in classes. For that, you need to use the **uk-subnav** class with the <ul> element. Let's understand this by a simple example in Listing 3-17.

Listing 3-17. Sub Navigation with Divider

```
<ul class="uk-subnav uk-subnav-divider" uk-margin>
    <li class="uk-active"><a href="#">Home</a></li>
    <li><a href="#">Profile</a></li>
    <li><a href="#">Notifications</a></li>
    <li><a href="#">Messages</a></li>
 </ul>
```

In Listing 3-17, we have created a list using the parent <ul> and child <li> items. We have assigned the **uk-subnav** class to define the sub navigation. We have also used the **uk-subnav-divider** class in tandem to create a divider between the items. Thereon, we have created a list just like in the previous examples using the <li> elements and <a> anchor tags within.

The output of the code is shown in Figure 3-16.

HOME   PROFILE   NOTIFICATIONS   MESSAGES

Figure 3-16. *Sub Navigation items*

In Figure 3-16, you can see that the sub navigation items are created with a divider in between them to differentiate the list items.

UIkit allows you to assign a background for the items using the pill modifier. Let's look at an example in Listing 3-18.

Listing 3-18. Sub Navigation with Pill Modifier

```
<ul class="uk-subnav uk-subnav-pill" uk-margin>
    <li class="uk-active"><a href="#">Home</a></li>
    <li><a href="#">Profile</a></li>
    <li><a href="#">Notifications</a></li>
        <li><a href="#">Messages</a></li>
</ul>
```

In Listing 3-18, we have used the <ul> elements and <li> elements the same way as in Listing 3-17. However, the difference here is that instead of the divider class, we have used the **uk-subnav-pill** class in tandem with the **uk-subnav** class. The rest of the code is the same as in Listing 3-17.

The output of the code is shown in Figure 3-17.

   PROFILE   NOTIFICATIONS   MESSAGES

Figure 3-17. *Sub Navigation with Pill Modifier*

In Figure 3-17, there is a background defined for the first pill. When you hover over the other pills, you can see a change in color akin to a gray shade.

Let's learn about Thumbnail navigation next.

Thumbnail Navigation

Thumbnail navigation is usually seen on websites nowadays. UIkit helps you create thumbnail navigation easily by using the **uk-thumbnav** class with the <ul> element as shown in Listing 3-19.

Listing 3-19. Thumbnail navigation

```
<ul class="uk-thumbnav" uk-margin>
    <li class="uk-active"><a href="#"><img src="Images/Chicago.
    jpg" width="90" alt="Chicago"></a></li>
    <li><a href="#"><img src="Images/London.jpg" width="90"
    alt="London"></a></li>
    <li><a href="#"><img src="Images/Madrid.jpg" width="90"
    alt="Madrid"></a></li>
        <li><a href="#"><img src="Images/New-York.jpg"
        width="90" alt="New-York"></a></li>
```

```
<li><a href="#"><img src="Images/Paris.jpg" width="90"
alt="Paris"></a></li>
</ul>
```

In Listing 3-19, we have used <ul>and <li> tags as the parent and child elements respectively. To the <ul> element, we have assigned the **uk-thumbnav** class, and also added a **uk-margin** attribute, which is quite handy if the items wrap up in the next row.

Thereon, we create five <li> elements within to create the list items. We use the image source wrapped within the <a> anchor tags. We assign the **uk-active** class to the first item to highlight it as the active item. We also define the width of the image as shown in the code.

The output of the code is shown in Figure 3-18.

Figure 3-18. *Thumbnail navigation*

In Figure 3-18, you can look at the thumbnail navigation and see that the first item is highlighted as the active item as defined in the code.

You can also create vertical thumb navigations in UIkit. For that, you need to use the **uk-thumbnav-vertical** class in conjunction with the **uk-thumbnav** class with the <ul> element as shown in Listing 3-20.

Listing 3-20. Vertically-aligned Thumb navigation

```
<ul class="uk-thumbnav uk-thumbnav-vertical" uk-margin>
    <li class="uk-active"><a href="#"><img src="Images/Chicago.
    jpg" width="90" alt="Chicago"></a></li>
    <li><a href="#"><img src="Images/London.jpg" width="90"
    alt="London"></a></li>
    <li><a href="#"><img src="Images/Madrid.jpg" width="90"
    alt="Madrid"></a></li>
    <li><a href="#"><img src="Images/New-York.jpg" width="90"
    alt="New-York"></a></li>
    <li><a href="#"><img src="Images/Paris.jpg" width="90"
    alt="Paris"></a></li>
</ul>
```

In Listing 3-20, we have used the same code as in Listing 3-19 except that we have used the **uk-thumbnav-vertical** class alongside the **uk-thumbnav** class. The rest of the code is the same.

The output of the code is shown in Figure 3-19.

Figure 3-19. *Vertically-aligned Thumbnail navigation*

In Figure 3-19, you can view the Thumbnail Navigation aligned vertically. The first item is active as defined in the code.

In the next section, we will look at the different types of media attributes.

Media Attributes

UIkit has many media attributes, some of which are explained in this chapter. We will look at Labels, Badges, Images, Carousels, and Slideshows in this section. So let's get started.

Labels

Labels indicate relevant and essential comments such as warnings, updates, and metadata information. UIkit comes with contextual classes for the Label feature.

Let's look at Listing 3-21 for an illustration of Labels.

Listing 3-21. Labels

```
<p class="uk-label">Sounds Good</p>
<br>
<p class="uk-label uk-label-success">Voila! You made it</p>
<br>
<p class="uk-label uk-label-warning">System Settings by
Administrators only</p>
<br>
<p class="uk-label uk-label-danger">Do not Delete</p>
```

In Listing 3-21, we have created four paragraph elements <p> and assigned the **uk-label** class to them. For the second, third, and final label classes, we have used the **uk-label-success**, **uk-label-warning**, and **uk-label-danger** classes in conjunction with the uk-label class respectively. This will indicate the contextual colors for the labels.

The output of the code is shown in Figure 3-20.

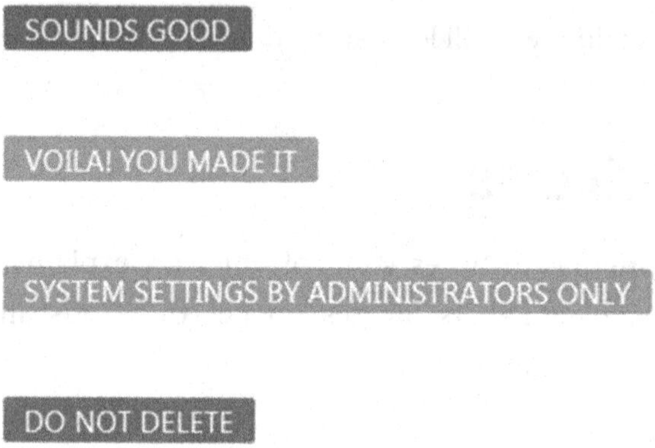

SOUNDS GOOD

VOILA! YOU MADE IT

SYSTEM SETTINGS BY ADMINISTRATORS ONLY

DO NOT DELETE

Figure 3-20. *Labels with contextual colors*

In Figure 3-20, you can see the labels with four different contextual colors as defined in the code.

Badges

Badges are extensively handy in social media and email clients to indicate a broad array of items such as notifications, unread messages, or some important information about some context.

Let's look at an example of items in Listing 3-22.

Listing 3-22. Badges

```
<ul uk-tab>
    <li><a href="">Home</a></li>
    <li><a href=""></a>Inbox</li>
        <li><a href=""></a>Profile</li>
        <li><a href="">Notifications <span class="uk-
        badge">33</span></a></li>
</ul>
```

In Listing 3-22, we have created a tab navigation as explained previously. We assigned the **uk-tab** attribute to the <ul> element. Then we created a list of items using the <li> tags as done before.

For the badges feature, in the last list item for notifications, we have added a <span> element and assigned it the **uk-badge** class within the anchor <a> tags.

The output of the code is shown in Figure 3-21.

HOME   Inbox   Profile   NOTIFICATIONS 33

Figure 3-21. *Badges*

In Figure 3-21, we can see that the last list item in the tab navigation, that is, *NOTIFICATIONS* has a badge indicating *33* as the notification count.

Carousels

UIkit has an ingrained performant carousel feature that can incorporate baked-in hardware-accelerated animations. The Carousel slider component is fully responsive and supports touch and swipe as well as mouse-drag attributes for desktops.

For this, you need to use the **uk-slider** attribute with the container elements and create a list of slider items using the **uk-slider-items** class. Let's look at an example in Listing 3-23. We will also be using the Slidenav component to create navigation with the previous and next buttons.

Listing 3-23. Carousel Slider

```
<div class="uk-position-relative uk-visible-toggle uk-light"
tabindex="-1" uk-slider>
    <ul class="uk-slider-items uk-child-width-1-3@s uk-child-
    width-1-4@m">
        <li>
            <img src="Images/New-York.jpg" alt="New York">
            <div class="uk-position-center uk-panel"><h1>New
            York</h1></div>
        </li>
        <li>
            <img src="Images/Paris.jpg" alt="Paris">
            <div class="uk-position-center uk-
            panel"><h1>Paris</h1></div>
        </li>
        <li>
            <img src="Images/London.jpg" alt="London">
            <div class="uk-position-center uk-
            panel"><h1>London</h1></div>
        </li>
        <li>
            <img src="Images/Chicago.jpg" alt="Chicago">
            <div class="uk-position-center uk-
            panel"><h1>Chicago</h1></div>
        </li>
        <li>
            <img src="Images/Madrid.jpg" alt="Madrid">
            <div class="uk-position-center uk-
            panel"><h1>Madrid</h1></div>
        </li>
    </ul>
```

```
<a class="uk-position-center-left uk-position-small uk-
hidden-hover uk-slidenav-large" href="#" uk-slidenav-
previous uk-slider-item="previous"></a>
<a class="uk-position-center-right uk-position-small uk-
hidden-hover uk-slidenav-large" href="#" uk-slidenav-next
uk-slider-item="next"></a>
</div>
```

In Listing 3-23, we assign the uk-slider attribute to a <div> element for activating the carousel slider component. For the <div> parent container, we assign the **uk-position-relative** class in conjunction with the **uk-light** class. The **uk-position-relative** class will apply relative positioning to the context. The **uk-light** class will improve the visibility of content and objects on dark backgrounds in a light style. In addition, we use the **uk-visible-toggle** class to display elements on hover or focus only.

You can also see *tabindex*= *-1* where **tabindex** defines the navigational order for the focusable elements and the **-1** value assigned to it allows it to receive programmatic focus, meaning focus can be set to it from a link or from scripting. Here, using *tabindex= "-1"* removes the element from the natural tab order.

Thereon, we create an unordered list using the <ul> and <li> elements. To the <ul> element, we assign the **uk-slider-items** class to invoke the slider items component. Then we assign a width to the carousel elements using the **uk-child-width-1-3@s** and **uk-child-width-1-4@m** classes, which will make the three slider items occupy a small screen and four slider items on medium-and-above sized screens respectively.

Then we create the five slider items by defining them under the <li> element tags. We introduce the images using the <img> elements. We also define a <div> element and assign the **uk-position-center** class alongside the **uk-panel** class to center the image in the positional context in a panel.

Finally, we create the slider navigation elements outside the <ul> tags. We use an anchor link <a> tag and assign the **uk-slidenav-previous** and **uk-slider-item="previous"** attributes to set the slider navigation for the previous slides. Then we also add the **uk-slidenav-large** classes to increase the size of the slider navigation buttons to large size. We also add the **uk-position-center-left** class to align the position of the slider navigation button. Next, we add the **uk-position-small** class to apply a small margin to the positioned slider navigation. Apart from that, we apply a **uk-hidden-hover** class so that the slider navigation is observed only while hovering over the slider items and not by default. Similarly, we create the slider navigation for the next button using the **slidenav-next** and **uk-slider-item="next"** attributes along with the **uk-position-center-right** class in another <a> element.

So, while hovering, the slider navigation button becomes visible. On hovering, you can see the slider navigation button, and you can click on it to see the slider items slide through the page as shown in Figure 3-22.

Figure 3-22. *Slider Carousel*

In Figure 3-22, you can see the slider items, that is, images of different cities; the slider buttons and name of the cities are in light color due to the uk-light attribute added to them. On hovering, the slider navigation buttons become visible as shown in the preceding screenshot, and you can click on them to see the items slide across the screen.

In UIkit, you can introduce a gap between the slider items using the uk-grid attribute and assigning it to the slider. The elements will then be spaced according to the default gap.

You can also introduce animations like autoplay, which will make the items slide without the need to click on the slide navigation buttons, meaning they will slide across the page automatically. You can also set an interval for that autoplay.

Let's see a slider carousel with a gap between the items and autoplay attribute in Listing 3-24.

Listing 3-24. Carousel slider with the Autoplay attribute

```
<div class="uk-position-relative uk-visible-toggle uk-light"
tabindex="-1" uk-slider="autoplay: true; autoplay-interval: 1000">
    <ul class="uk-slider-items uk-child-width-1-3@s uk-child-
    width-1-4@m uk-grid">
        <li>
            <img src="Images/New-York.jpg" alt="New York">
            <div class="uk-position-center uk-panel"><h1>
            New York</h1></div>
        </li>
        <li>
            <img src="Images/Paris.jpg" alt="Paris">
            <div class="uk-position-center uk-
            panel"><h1>Paris</h1></div>
        </li>
        <li>
            <img src="Images/London.jpg" alt="London">
            <div class="uk-position-center uk-panel">
            <h1>London</h1></div>
        </li>
        <li>
            <img src="Images/Chicago.jpg" alt="Chicago">
            <div class="uk-position-center uk-panel"><h1>
            Chicago</h1></div>
        </li>
```

```
    <li>
        <img src="Images/Madrid.jpg" alt="Madrid">
        <div class="uk-position-center uk-panel">
        <h1>Madrid</h1></div>
    </li>
</ul>
<a class="uk-position-center-left uk-position-small
uk-hidden-hover uk-slidenav-large" href="#" uk-slidenav-
previous uk-slider-item="previous"></a>
<a class="uk-position-center-right uk-position-small
uk-hidden-hover uk-slidenav-large" href="#" uk-slidenav-
next uk-slider-item="next"></a>
</div>
```

In Listing 3-24, we have used similar code as in the previous normal carousel slider, but here we have introduced an autoplay animation by assigning the **autoplay: true** property with the **uk-slider** attribute, which will activate the slides to move across the screen automatically. We have also added the **autoplay-interval: 1000** property to the slider attribute, which will enable the sliding action every 1000 ms.

Then, we have used the same code for the child <ul> element within the <div> element, but here we have used the **uk-grid** attribute as highlighted in the code. This will introduce the gap between the slider items – in this case, the images.

The rest of the code is the same as the normal carousel slider in the earlier listing.

The output of the code is shown in Figure 3-23.

Figure 3-23. *Autoplay Carousel slider images with Gaps*

In Figure 3-23, you can see the images have a gap between them and the five images slide across the screen at an interval of 1000 ms.

If you need to stop the autoplay, you need to hover over the image, where you can see the slider navigation buttons, and you can slide them manually. The moment you stop hovering, the images start sliding again automatically as per the autoplay property.

In the next section, we will look at the Slideshow component.

Slideshow

UIkit has an ingrained performant Slideshow feature that can incorporate baked-in hardware-accelerated animations. The Slideshow component is fully responsive and supports touch and swipe as well as mouse-drag attributes for desktops.

For using the Slideshow feature, you need to assign the **uk-slideshow** attribute to the container element. You can create the slider items using the **uk-slideshow-items** class.

Listing 3-25 shows an illustration of a normal slideshow.

Listing 3-25. Slideshow feature

```
<div class="uk-position-relative uk-visible-toggle uk-light"
tabindex="-1" uk-slideshow>
    <ul class="uk-slideshow-items">
        <li>
            <img src="images/New-York.jpg" alt="New York"
            uk-cover>
        </li>
        <li>
            <img src="images/Chicago.jpg" alt="Chicago"
            uk-cover>
        </li>
```

```
<li>
    <img src="images/London.jpg" alt="London" uk-cover>
</li>
        <li>
    <img src="images/Madrid.jpg" alt="Madrid" uk-cover>
</li>
        <li>
    <img src="images/Paris.jpg" alt="Paris" uk-cover>
</li>
</ul>
<a class="uk-position-center-left uk-position-small
uk-hidden-hover uk-slidenav-large" href="#" uk-slidenav-
previous uk-slideshow-item="previous"></a>
<a class="uk-position-center-right uk-position-small
uk-hidden-hover uk-slidenav-large" href="#" uk-slidenav-
next uk-slideshow-item="next"></a>
</div>
```

Here, in Listing 3-25, we create a parent <div> container and assign the **uk-position-relative** class alongside the **uk-visible-toggle** and **uk-light** classes just like in the case of the carousel element. The functionality is the same as explained in the carousel element. But here, we use the **uk-slideshow** attribute to invoke the slideshow component.

Thereon, we create five list items using the <ul> and <li> elements. We assign the **uk-slideshow-items** class to the <ul> element. We use the **uk-cover** attribute with the <img> tag to add the image in the background of each slide within the <li> elements.

Finally, we create the slider navigation elements outside the <ul> tags. We use an anchor link <a> tag and assign the **uk-slidenav-previous** and **uk-slideshow-item="previous"** attributes to set the slider navigation for the previous slides. Then we also add the **uk-slidenav-large** classes to increase the size of the slider navigation to a large size. We also add the **uk-position-center-left** class to align the position of the slider navigation button. Next, we add the **uk-position-small** class to apply a small margin to the positioned slider navigation. Apart from that, we apply a **uk-hidden-hover** class so that the slider navigation is observed only while hovering over the slider items and not by default. Similarly, we create the slider navigation for the next button using the **slidenav-next** and **uk-slideshow-item="next"** attributes along with the **uk-position-center-right** class in another <a> element.

The output of the code will show the first image as defined in the code. When you hover over the images, you can see the slider navigation buttons. You can shift from slide to slide using the slider navigation arrows.

Figure 3-24 shows the first slide that appears on executing the code.

Figure 3-24. *Slideshow feature*

By default, a slide animation is set by default in UIkit. You can introduce Animation effects by invoking the animation component in UIkit.

Let's see an illustration of that in Listing 3-26.

Listing 3-26. Animation Scale feature in Slideshow

```
<div class="uk-position-relative uk-visible-toggle uk-light"
tabindex="-1" uk-slideshow="animation: scale">
    <ul class="uk-slideshow-items">
        <li>
            <img src="images/New-York.jpg" alt="New York" uk-
            cover>
        </li>
        <li>
            <img src="images/Chicago.jpg" alt="Chicago" uk-
            cover>
        </li>
        <li>
            <img src="images/London.jpg" alt="London" uk-cover>
        </li>
            <li>
            <img src="images/Madrid.jpg" alt="Madrid" uk-cover>
        </li>
            <li>
            <img src="images/Paris.jpg" alt="Paris" uk-cover>
        </li>
    </ul>
    <a class="uk-position-center-left uk-position-small uk-
    hidden-hover uk-slidenav-large" href="#" uk-slidenav-
    previous uk-slideshow-item="previous"></a>
    <a class="uk-position-center-right uk-position-small uk-
    hidden-hover uk-slidenav-large" href="#" uk-slidenav-next
    uk-slideshow-item="next"></a>
</div>
```

In Listing 3-26, we have used the same code as in Listing 3-25, but we have introduced an animation feature by assigning the **animation: scale** property to the **uk-slideshow** attribute. The rest of the code is the same as in Listing 3-25.

The output of the code will result in the slides scaling up whenever you click on the slide navigation button. (You can also use other animations like Fade to the mix-up depending on your requirements – more on that in Chapter 4.)

The output of the code on scaling to the next image is shown in Figure 3-25 (it is in the process of the scaling effect and not rendered completely).

Figure 3-25. *Scaling effect in SlideShow rendering the next image*

You can also add the *Ken Burns* effect to the Slideshow. (*The Ken Burns effect is a type of panning and zooming effect used in video production from still imagery. The name derives from extensive use of the technique by American documentarian Ken Burns.* Source: https://en.wikipedia. org/wiki/Ken_Burns_effect)

To create a Ken Burns effect, let's look at Listing 3-27.

Listing 3-27. Kenburns effect on Slideshow

```
<div class="uk-position-relative uk-visible-toggle uk-light"
tabindex="-1" uk-slideshow="animation: scale">
    <ul class="uk-slideshow-items">
        <li>
                <div class="uk-position-cover uk-animation-
                kenburns">
            <img src="images/New-York.jpg" alt="New York"
            uk-cover>
        </div>
                </li>
        <li>
                <div class="uk-position-cover uk-animation-
                kenburns">
            <img src="images/Chicago.jpg" alt="Chicago"
            uk-cover>
        </div>
                </li>
        <li>
                <div class="uk-position-cover uk-animation-
                kenburns">
            <img src="images/London.jpg" alt="London" uk-cover>
        </div>
                </li>
                 <li>
                <div class="uk-position-cover uk-animation-
                kenburns">
            <img src="images/Madrid.jpg" alt="Madrid" uk-cover>
        </div>
                </li>
```

```
        <li>
        <div class="uk-position-cover uk-animation-
        kenburns">
    <img src="images/Paris.jpg" alt="Paris" uk-cover>
  </div>
        </li>
</ul>
<a class="uk-position-center-left uk-position-small uk-
hidden-hover uk-slidenav-large" href="#" uk-slidenav-
previous uk-slideshow-item="previous"></a>
<a class="uk-position-center-right uk-position-small uk-
hidden-hover uk-slidenav-large" href="#" uk-slidenav-next
uk-slideshow-item="next"></a>
```
</div>

In Listing 3-27, we have used the same scaling effect Animation code we have used in the previous Listing 3-26, except for a few changes. We have wrapped the image with a <div> element and assigned the **uk-animation-kenburns** and **uk-position-cover** classes to it.

The **uk-animation-kenburns** class invokes the animation effect whereas the **uk-position-cover** class will enable the position element to cover its container.

The output of the code will result in a zooming effect, where the picture will become larger as per the animation. Here we have used scale as the animation, and it will scale and appear to zoom larger as shown in Figure 3-26.

Figure 3-26. *Ken Burns effect in Slideshows*

When you click on the Slide navigation button, the scale animation will be activated and the image will zoom and become larger, that is, demonstrating the Ken Burns effect. You can use different animations other than scale too in UIkit.

Summary

In this chapter, we looked at the navigation elements and media attributes in UIkit. We learned about several elements such as dropdowns, list navigations, tabbed navigations, and thumbnail navigations to name a few. We saw the different media attributes such as Labels, Badges, Carousel Sliders, and Slideshows with their different attributes. In the next chapter, we will look at UIkit's CSS components, which help create intuitive designs with relative ease.

CHAPTER 4

Active CSS and JavaScript Components

The very reason for using a CSS framework is to use its integrated user-interface elements, which makes it easier to develop complex websites. In addition to CSS Components, UIkit comes bundled with JavaScript elements to add intricate functionality. We will learn about the following components in this chapter:

- Buttons

- Icons

- Accordions

- Alerts

- Tooltips

- Modals

- Panels

- Tiles

- Upload

- Inverse

© Aravind Shenoy 2020
A. Shenoy, *Jumpstart UIKit*, https://doi.org/10.1007/978-1-4842-6029-6_4

- Visibility

- Pagination

- Animations

- Transitions

Buttons

UIkit is batteries-included and comprises several types of buttons and button groups. All you need to do is add the **uk-button** class in tandem with the **uk-button-default** class to an anchor <a> or <button> element to create a button. The difference is that if the button links to a different page or is a link to an anchor, then we use the <a> tags, or if you want to alter something on the same page, we use the <button> tags.

Normal Buttons

Let's look at Listing 4-1 to see a normal button.

Listing 4-1. Normal buttons

```
<p uk-margin>
    <a class="uk-button uk-button-default" href="#">Click
    Here</a>
    <button class="uk-button uk-button-default">Click Here
    </button>
</p>
```

In Listing 4-1, we have the <p> paragraph element and assigned the **uk-margin** class to it. This will create the necessary top spacing between the buttons when they are stacked on smaller viewports. Then, we use the <a> tags and assign the **uk-button** and **uk-button-default** class to it.

Next, we create a similar button, but here we use the <button> tags with the same classes as the previous <a> tags.

The output of the code is shown in Figure 4-1.

Figure 4-1. *Normal Buttons*

In Figure 4-1, you can see both the normal buttons created using the <a> and <button> elements.

Contextual-Colored Buttons

You can add contextual colors to the buttons using the **uk-button-primary**, **uk-button-secondary**, and **uk-button-danger** classes. You can also use the **disabled** attribute to create a disabled button. Listing 4-2 shows an illustration of the same.

Listing 4-2. Contextual-Colored buttons

```
<p uk-margin>
  <button class="uk-button uk-button-primary">Click Here
  </button>
  <button class="uk-button uk-button-secondary">Click Here
  </button>
  <button class="uk-button uk-button-danger">Click Here
  </button>
  <button class="uk-button uk-button-default" disabled>
  Click Here</button>
</p>
```

In Listing 4-2, we have used the primary, secondary, danger, and default button classes. We have used the **disabled** attribute with the default button.

The output of the code is shown in Figure 4-2.

Figure 4-2. *Contextual-colored buttons and Disabled button*

Different-Sized Buttons

UIkit allows you to create small- and large-sized buttons using the **uk-button-small** and **uk-button-large** classes (we have already seen the default normal-sized buttons earlier). Refer to Listing 4-3 to see an illustration.

Listing 4-3. Small- and Large-sized buttons

```
<p uk-margin>
    <button class="uk-button uk-button-primary uk-button-
    small">Click Here</button>
    <br><br>
    <button class="uk-button uk-button-secondary uk-button-
    large">Click Here</button>
</p>
```

In Listing 4-3, we have created two buttons, one small and the other large, by using the **uk-button-small** and **uk-button-large** classes. We have used the primary and secondary contextual colors for the buttons respectively.

The output of the code is shown in Figure 4-3.

Figure 4-3. *Small- and Large-sized buttons*

Button Width Modifiers

You can define the width of the buttons by using width modifiers. Refer to Listing 4-4 to see an illustration.

Listing 4-4. Button Width Modifiers

```
<div>
    <div>
        <button class="uk-button uk-button-danger uk-button-
        large uk-width-1-1">Eat</button>
        <br><br>
        <button class="uk-button uk-button-primary uk-button-
        large uk-width-1-2">Sleep</button>
        <br><br>
        <button class="uk-button uk-button-secondary uk-button-
        large uk-width-5-6">Rave</button>
        <br><br>
    <button class="uk-button uk-button-default uk-button-large
    uk-width-3-4">Repeat</button>
    </div>
</div>
```

In Listing 4-4, we create four large buttons and use the contextual colors to distinguish the buttons. Then we define the **uk-width-1-1**, **uk-width-1-2**, **uk-width-5-6**, and **uk-width-3-4** classes for the four buttons, due to which buttons will take up their respective widths.

The output of the code is shown in Figure 4-4.

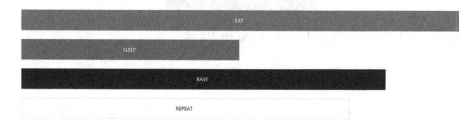

Figure 4-4. *Different width modifiers*

In Figure 4-4, you can see that the first button has taken full width, whereas the second, third, and fourth buttons have taken half-width, five-sixths width, and three-fourths widths as defined in the code.

Grouped Buttons

Grouped buttons are an excellent utility as you can group buttons in a single bar to perform a group of actions, such as Create, View, Update, and Delete. Listing 4-5 shows an illustration of the same.

Listing 4-5. Button Groups

```
<p uk-margin>
    <div class="uk-button-group">
        <button class="uk-button uk-button-primary">
        Create</button>
        <button class="uk-button uk-button-secondary">View
        </button>
```

```
    <button class="uk-button uk-button-danger">Update
    </button>
    <button class="uk-button uk-button-default">Delete
    </button>
  </div>
</p>
```

In Listing 4-5, we have created a button group of *Create, View, Update,* and *Delete* buttons. Initially, we use a parent <div> to which we have assigned the **uk-button-group** class. Then we define four buttons with different contextual colors using the <button> elements.

The output of the code is shown in Figure 4-5.

Figure 4-5. *Grouped buttons*

So we saw the different button attributes in this section. In the next section, we will look at the different icon attributes.

Icons

UIkit has an ingrained, extensive SVG Icons library, which can be injected in the site and styled easily with CSS. For that, we have used the following CDN icon library script in the <head> tag.

```
<script src="https://cdn.jsdelivr.net/npm/uikit@3.3.0/dist/js/
uikit-icons.min.js"></script>
```

Normal Icons

Let's get started with icons directly as illustrated in Listing 4-6.

Listing 4-6. Normal Icons

```
<span class="uk-margin-small-right" uk-icon="home"></span>
<span class="uk-margin-small-right" uk-icon="user"></span>
<span class="uk-margin-small-right" uk-icon="cloud-
upload"></span>
<span class="uk-margin-small-right" uk-icon="download"></span>
<span class="uk-margin-small-right" uk-icon="trash"></span>
<span uk-icon="sign-out"></span>
```

In Listing 4-6, we have six <span> elements and used the **uk-margin-small-right** class to include spacing between the icons. Then we define the icons using the **uk-icon** attribute. We have assigned six different icons, namely - home, user, cloud-upload, download, trash, and sign out.

The output of the code is shown in Figure 4-6.

Figure 4-6. *Normal Icons*

Icons with Ratio Modifiers

You can increase the size of the icons with ratio modifiers. Refer to Listing 4-7 to see an illustration of the same.

Listing 4-7. Ratio Modifiers icons

```
<span class="uk-margin-small-right" uk-icon="home"></span>
<span class="uk-margin-small-right" uk-icon="user"></span>
<span class="uk-margin-small-right" uk-icon="cloud-upload"></span>
<span class="uk-margin-small-right" uk-icon="download"></span>
```

```
<span class="uk-margin-small-right" uk-icon="trash"></span>
<span uk-icon="sign-out"></span>
    <br><br><br>
<span class="uk-margin-small-right" uk-icon="icon: home;
ratio: 2"></span>
<span class="uk-margin-small-right" uk-icon="icon: user;
ratio: 2"></span>
<span class="uk-margin-small-right" uk-icon="icon: cloud-
upload; ratio: 2"></span>
<span class="uk-margin-small-right" uk-icon="icon: download;
ratio: 2"></span>
<span class="uk-margin-small-right" uk-icon="icon: trash;
ratio: 2"></span>
<span uk-icon="icon: sign-out; ratio: 2"></span>
```

In Listing 4-7, we have used the normal icons first as defined in
Listing 4-6.

In the second section of the code, we have used the **ratio: 2** value in
conjunction with the defined icons assigned to the **uk-icon** attribute.

The output of the code is shown in Figure 4-7.

Figure 4-7. *Comparison of normal and ratio-modified icons*

In Figure 4-7, you can see that the icons below are twice the size,
significantly bigger than the first set of icons.

Social Media Icons

For social media icon buttons, you need to use the **uk-icon-button** class in conjunction with the **uk-icon** attribute. Refer to Listing 4-8 to see an illustration.

Listing 4-8. Social Media Buttons

```
<a href="" class="uk-icon-button uk-margin-small-right"
uk-icon="google"></a>
  <a href="" class="uk-icon-button uk-margin-small-right"
  uk-icon="instagram"></a>
  <a href="" class="uk-icon-button uk-margin-small-right"
  uk-icon="twitter"></a>
  <a href="" class="uk-icon-button uk-margin-small-right"
  uk-icon="facebook"></a>
  <a href="" class="uk-icon-button uk-margin-small-right"
  uk-icon="linkedin"></a>
  <a href="" class="uk-icon-button" uk-icon="youtube"></a>
```

In Listing 4-8, we have used the **uk-icon-button** class in conjunction with the **uk-margin-small-right** class. Then we have defined the Google, Instagram, Twitter, Facebook, LinkedIn, and YouTube icons using the **uk-icon** attribute (in this example, instead of the <span> tags, we have used the <a> elements).

The output of the code is shown in Figure 4-8.

Figure 4-8. *Social Media Buttons*

Now that we are familiar with icons in UIkit, we will look at Accordion panels in the next section.

Accordions

Accordions help you encapsulate sizable content in a compact area. UIkit's accordions are styled like a stack of collapsible panels and act on a multilevel menu. By default, they have a menu-collapsible feature when you click on a new panel.

In UIkit, you use the **uk-accordion** attribute to define an accordion. Thereon, we use the **uk-accordion-title** class to define the feel and toggle of an accordion item. The **uk-accordion-content** class is used to define the content in the panel.

Let's look at an illustration in Listing 4-9 (remember that we have used the entire sample content in the code bundle but in the example in the book we are just jotting down three words followed by …).

Listing 4-9. Accordions

```
<ul uk-accordion>
    <li class="uk-open">
        <a class="uk-accordion-title" href="#"> OPEN UNO </a>
        <div class="uk-accordion-content">
            <p>Cat ipsum dolor.... </p>
        </div>
    </li>
    <li>
        <a class="uk-accordion-title" href="#"> OPEN DUOS </a>
        <div class="uk-accordion-content">
            <p>Nequeporro totam and ullam... .</p>
        </div>
    </li>
  </ul>
```

In Listing 4-9, we have used the list <ul> tag and defined two child <li> elements to define the panels of the accordion. We assign the **uk-accordion** attribute to the <ul> element. For the first <li> element, we assign the **uk-open** class, due to the panel open displaying the content within. Then we use an anchor <a> element and assign the **uk-accordion-title** class to it. Within that, we create a <div> element, to which we assign the **uk-accordion-content** class. We define the content within that <div> using <p> tags.

Similarly, we create the second <li> element, but we do not use the **uk-open** class to it because it will be closed by default. We define the classes the same way, but we use different content in the panel.

The output of the code is shown in Figure 4-9.

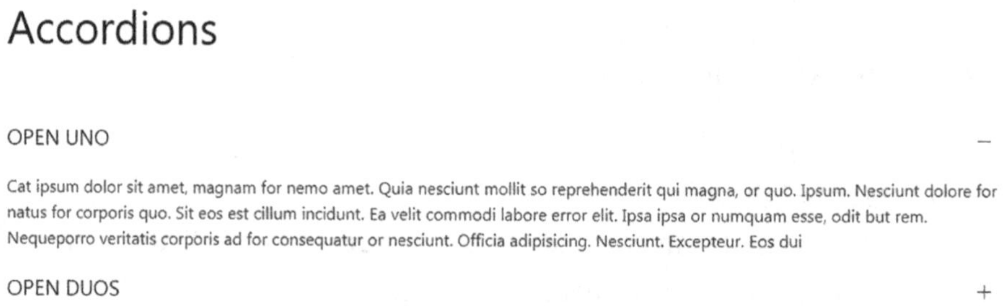

Accordions

OPEN UNO   —

Cat ipsum dolor sit amet, magnam for nemo amet. Quia nesciunt mollit so reprehenderit qui magna, or quo. Ipsum. Nesciunt dolore for natus for corporis quo. Sit eos est cillum incidunt. Ea velit commodi labore error elit. Ipsa ipsa or numquam esse, odit but rem. Nequeporro veritatis corporis ad for consequatur or nesciunt. Officia adipisicing. Nesciunt. Excepteur. Eos dui

OPEN DUOS   +

Figure 4-9. *Accordions*

In Figure 4-9, the first panel is open as defined in the code. The second accordion panel is closed and will open up when we click on the plus sign at the right of the panel. However, the first panel will close once the lower one is opened.

To have multiple panels open, we need to assign the **multiple: true** value to the **uk-accordion attribute**. Listing 4-10 shows an example of the same.

Listing 4-10. Multiple Accordion Panels

```
<ul uk-accordion="multiple: true">
    <li class="uk-open">
        <a class="uk-accordion-title" href="#"> OPEN UNO </a>
        <div class="uk-accordion-content">
            <p>Cat ipsum dolor sit...</p>
        </div>
    </li>
    <li>
        <a class="uk-accordion-title" href="#"> OPEN DUOS </a>
        <div class="uk-accordion-content">
            <p>Nequeporro totam and ullam ... Minima</p>
        </div>
    </li>
```

In Listing 4-10, we have assigned the **multiple: true** value to the **uk-accordion** attribute - the rest of the code is the same as Listing 4-9.

Now on executing the code, the first panel content will be displayed due to the **uk-open** class assigned to it. But when we click on the plus sign of the first panel, the content of the second panel will be displayed - but the first panel will not collapse and will display the content within it in tandem with the second panel content.

The output of the code on opening the second panel is shown in Figure 4-10.

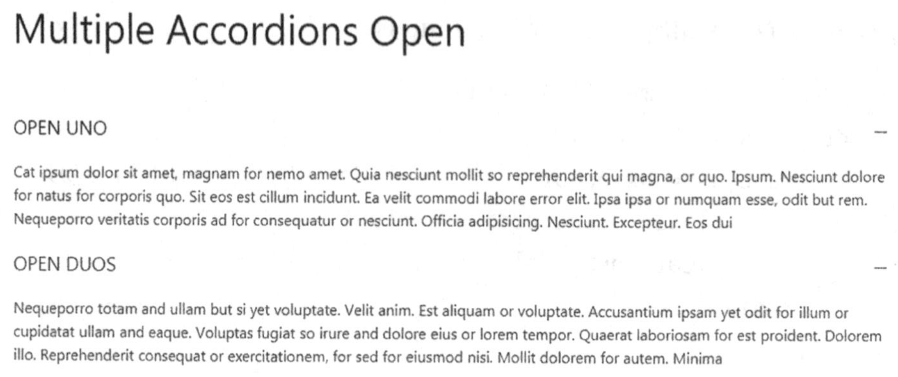

Multiple Accordions Open

OPEN UNO   —

Cat ipsum dolor sit amet, magnam for nemo amet. Quia nesciunt mollit so reprehenderit qui magna, or quo. Ipsum. Nesciunt dolore for natus for corporis quo. Sit eos est cillum incidunt. Ea velit commodi labore error elit. Ipsa ipsa or numquam esse, odit but rem. Nequeporro veritatis corporis ad for consequatur or nesciunt. Officia adipisicing. Nesciunt. Excepteur. Eos dui

OPEN DUOS   —

Nequeporro totam and ullam but si yet voluptate. Velit anim. Est aliquam or voluptate. Accusantium ipsam yet odit for illum or cupidatat ullam and eaque. Voluptas fugiat so irure and dolore eius or lorem tempor. Quaerat laboriosam for est proident. Dolorem illo. Reprehenderit consequat or exercitationem, for sed for eiusmod nisi. Mollit dolorem for autem. Minima

Figure 4-10. *Multiple Accordion panels open*

Now that we looked at a few Accordion attributes, we will look at Alerts in the next section.

Alerts

UIkit lets you define alerts, which makes users aware of imperative information related to their current activity. All you need to do is add the **uk-alert** attribute to an element to define an alert as shown in Listing 4-11. You can also define contextual colors to the alerts in UIkit.

Listing 4-11. Contextual alert boxes

```
<div>
     <h3>
     <u>Alerts</u>
     </h3>
   </div>
<div uk-alert>
<p>Accusantium ipsam yet odit for illum or cupidatat ullam and
eaque. Voluptas fugiat so irureswe</p>
</div>
```

116

```
<div class="uk-alert-primary" uk-alert>
<p>Laboriosam labore and eum inventore yet quae and ullamco
dicta. In velitesse and anim alerios </p>
</div>
<div class="uk-alert-success" uk-alert>
<p>totam. Aliqua autem and adipisci yet ut, so ex. Natus rem
suscipit nesciunt so fugiat, ale voluire</p>
</div>
<div class="uk-alert-warning" uk-alert>
<p>Minima amet exercitation but aperiam aliquid irure or ex.
Consectetur labore so ratione ale for</p>
</div>
<div class="uk-alert-danger" uk-alert>
 <p>Cillum numquam, or velit quo corporis, laboris modi. Labore
doloremque for consequuratione </p>
</div>
```

In Listing 4-11, we have defined five <div> elements for the alerts.
We have assigned the **uk-alert** attribute for each <div> element. Then,
we have assigned the **uk-alert-primary**, **uk-alert-success**, **uk-alert-
warning**, and **uk-alert-danger** classes to the second, third, fourth, and
fifth <div> elements in conjunction with the **uk-alert** attribute.

The output of the code is shown in Figure 4-11.

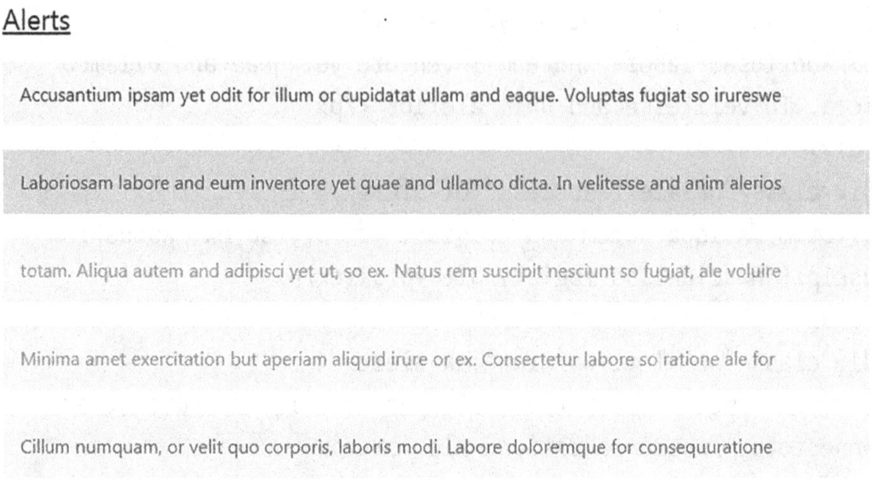

Alerts

Accusantium ipsam yet odit for illum or cupidatat ullam and eaque. Voluptas fugiat so irureswe

Laboriosam labore and eum inventore yet quae and ullamco dicta. In velitesse and anim alerios

totam. Aliqua autem and adipisci yet ut, so ex. Natus rem suscipit nesciunt so fugiat, ale voluire

Minima amet exercitation but aperiam aliquid irure or ex. Consectetur labore so ratione ale for

Cillum numquam, or velit quo corporis, laboris modi. Labore doloremque for consequuratione

Figure 4-11. *Contextual-colored Alerts*

To create a close button for each alert, you can create an anchor tag within each <div> defining the alert box and assign the **uk-alert-close** class to it. Then you need to add the **uk-close** attribute in conjunction to invoke the close component.

Listing 4-12 shows an illustration of the same.

Listing 4-12. Contextual alert boxes with close functionality

```
<div>
     <h2>
     <u>Alerts</u>
     </h2>
   </div>
<div uk-alert>
<a class="uk-alert-close" uk-close></a>
<p>Accusantium ipsam yet odit for illum or cupidatat ullam and
eaque. Voluptas fugiat so irureswe</p>
</div>
```

```
<div class="uk-alert-primary" uk-alert>
 <a class="uk-alert-close" uk-close></a>
<p>Laboriosam labore and eum inventore yet quae and ullamco
dicta. In velitesse and anim alerios </p>
</div>
<div class="uk-alert-success" uk-alert>
 <a class="uk-alert-close" uk-close></a>
 <p>totam. Aliqua autem and adipisci yet ut, so ex. Natus rem
 suscipit nesciunt so fugiat, ale voluire</p>
 </div>
 <div class="uk-alert-warning" uk-alert>
 <a class="uk-alert-close" uk-close></a>
 <p>Minima amet exercitation but aperiam aliquid irure or ex.
 Consectetur labore so ratione ale for</p>
 </div>
<div class="uk-alert-danger" uk-alert>
<a class="uk-alert-close" uk-close></a>
 <p>Cillum numquam, or velit quo corporis, laboris modi. Labore
 doloremque for consequuratione </p>
</div>
```

In Listing 4-12, we have used the same code as in Listing 4-11, except we have introduced an anchor <a> tag within each parent <div> for each alert box and assigned the **uk-alert** close class in conjunction with the **uk-close** attribute.

The output of the code is shown in Figure 4-12.

Alerts

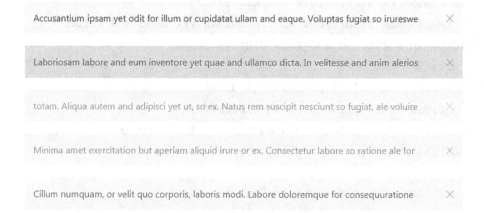

Figure 4-12. Alert Boxes with close functionality

In the next section, we will learn about Tooltips in UIkit.

Tooltips

Tooltips are labels displayed when you hover over an element. UIkit helps you create tooltips by using the **uk-tooltip** attribute. Let's understand this by an example in Listing 4-13.

Listing 4-13. Tooltips

```
<button class="uk-button uk-button-primary" uk-tooltip="Whazz
up">Click Here</button>
```

In Listing 4-13, we have created a primary button (*Click Here*) and assigned the **uk-tooltip** attribute to it. Then we have defined the value *Whazz up* to the **uk-tooltip** attribute. When you execute the code, you will see a *Click Here* button. On hovering over the button, you will see the *Whazz up* label.

The output of the code on hovering is shown in Figure 4-13.

Figure 4-13. *Tooltip on hover*

You can also align the tooltip to the top, right, top-left, top-right, bottom, bottom-left, bottom-right, and left using the following attribute values:

- pos: top Aligns the tooltip to the top.

- pos: top-left Aligns the tooltip to the top left.

- pos: top-right Aligns the tooltip to the top right.

- pos: bottom Aligns the tooltip to the bottom.

- pos: bottom-left Aligns the tooltip to the bottom left.

- pos: bottom-right Aligns the tooltip to the bottom right.

- pos: left Aligns the tooltip to the left.

- pos: right Aligns the tooltip to the right.

You can also introduce a delay for the tooltip so that it appears after the defined time in milliseconds.

Let's look at an example in Listing 4-14.

Listing 4-14. Tooltip positioning and delay

```
<button class="uk-button uk-button-primary" uk-tooltip="title:
HEY JOE COOL!; pos: right; delay: 1000">TO THE RIGHT</button>
```

In Listing 4-14, we have created a primary button. We have assigned a **uk-tooltip** attribute to it. Since we are introducing positioning of the tooltip to the right with a delay of *1000 ms*, we assign the **title** property to

121

the **uk-tooltip** attribute and assign a value *HEY JOE COOL!* to it. Then separated by a semicolon, we assign the **pos: right** property to it followed by the **delay: 1000** property.

What **pos: right** does is assign the tooltip to the right - whereas the **delay: 1000** will make the tooltip appear after a period of 1000 ms.

The output of the code is shown in Figure 4-14.

Figure 4-14. *Right positioning of tooltip with delay*

In the next section, we are going to look at Modals and different types of overlays.

Modals

Using Modals, one can overlay an element over a website. You can see the information without having to leave the webpage you are viewing. It enhances the usability and accounts for good aesthetics.

UIkit has capabilities that allow you to create modals without much markup.

Normal Modals

Listing 4-15 shows an example of normal modals with a header, body, and footer (remember that we have used sample content in the code bundle, but in the example in the book we are just jotting down few words followed by ...).

Listing 4-15. Modals with header, body, and footer

```
<button class="uk-button uk-button-primary" href="#my-modal"
uk-toggle>Click Here</button>
<div id="my-modal" uk-modal>
    <div class="uk-modal-dialog">
        <button class="uk-modal-close-default" type="button"
        uk-close></button>
        <div class="uk-modal-header">
            <h2 class="uk-modal-title">CAT IPSUM</h2>
        </div>
        <div class="uk-modal-body">
            <p>Cat ipsum dolor sit amet, cougar for puma and
            ragdoll or bobcat...</p>
        </div>
        <div class="uk-modal-footer uk-text-right">
        <button class="uk-button uk-button-danger uk-modal-
        close">Exit</button>
            <button class="uk-button uk-button-
            secondary">Save</button>
        </div>
    </div>
</div>
```

First, we create a primary button and add the **uk-toggle** attribute to it. The **uk-toggle** attribute activates the JavaScript to toggle a modal dialog. We also use an **href** attribute to which we assign a *my-modal* value. This value will be referenced by the id of the <div> element where we define the modal.

Then we create that parent <div> and assign it an id. The value of that id would be *my-modal*, which we had used with the <button> element. Then we assign the **uk-modal** attribute to it.

Within that parent <div>, we create a child <div> to which we assign the **uk-modal-dialog** class to create a dialog. Thereon, we create a close button using the <button> element within the child <div>. To the button, we assign the **uk-modal-close-default** class. We also invoke the close functionality by assigning the **uk-close** attribute.

Next, we create the Modal header. We create a child <div> within the child <div>. We assign the **uk-modal-header** class to it. Then we define a heading for the modal and assign the **uk-modal-title** class to it, thereby creating the modal title.

Next, we create another <div> and define the modal body. We assign the **uk-modal-body** class to it to create padding between the modal and its respective content. Then we define the body content in the modal body within the <p> element.

Finally, we define the modal footer. We create another <div> and assign the **uk-modal-footer** and **uk-text-right** classes to it so that the modal footer is created and the text is aligned to the right.

Then we create two buttons, *Exit* and *Save*, one with the danger contextual color and the other with the secondary contextual color respectively. To both of the buttons, we assign the **type** attribute as **button**. We assign the **uk-modal-close** attribute to the *Exit* button so that you can exit the modal by clicking on it.

The output of the code will result in a *Click Here* button, which on clicking will result in the overlay, as shown in Figure 4-15.

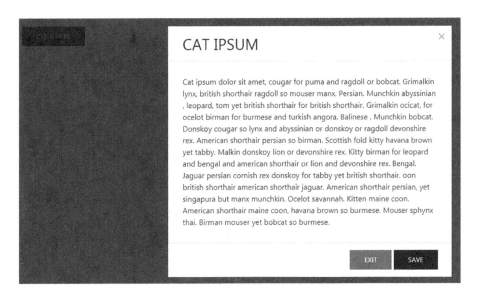

Figure 4-15. *Modal Overlay*

You can also create full-width modals, which we are going to look at in the next section.

Full-Width Modals

We use the same code as in Listing 4-15. But we will be using the *uk-modal-full* class with the parent div element as shown in Listing 4-16. We also increased the text of the sample content so that it spans the entire page.

Listing 4-16. Full-Width Modals

```
<button class="uk-button uk-button-primary" href="#my-modal"
uk-toggle>Click Here</button>
<div id="my-modal" class="uk-modal-full" uk-modal>
    <div class="uk-modal-dialog">
        <button class="uk-modal-close-default" type="button"
        uk-close></button>
```

```
<div class="uk-modal-header">
    <h2 class="uk-modal-title">CAT IPSUM </h2>
</div>
<div class="uk-modal-body">
    <p>Cat ipsum dolor sit amet, cougar for puma and
    ragdoll or bobcat. Grimalkin... </p>
</div>
<div class="uk-modal-footer uk-text-right">
    <button class="uk-button uk-button-danger uk-modal-
    close" type="button">Exit</button>
    <button class="uk-button uk-button-secondary"
    type="button">Save</button>
</div>
    </div>
</div>
```

The output of the code will result in a *Click Here* button, which on clicking will display the full-width modal. The modal overlay in this case will occupy the full width of the entire page as shown in Figure 4-16.

Figure 4-16. *Full-Width Modals*

In the next section, we will look at Image Modals.

Image Modals

UIkit lets you define media modals wherein you can use images and videos as overlays. Listing 4-17 shows an illustration of the same.

Listing 4-17. Image Modals

```
<p uk-margin>
<a class="uk-button uk-button-primary" href="#modal-image" uk-
toggle>Shrek</a>
</p>
<div id="modal-image" class="uk-flex-top" uk-modal>
    <div class="uk-modal-dialog uk-width-auto uk-margin-auto-
    vertical">
        <button class="uk-modal-close-outside" type="button"
        uk-close></button>
        <img src="Images/Shrek.png" width="500" height="500"
        alt="Shrek">
    </div>
</div>
```

In Listing 4-17, we have created a paragraph <p> element, to which we have assigned a **uk-margin** attribute to introduce spacing. Within the <p> tags, we have created a primary button and assigned a **href** attribute to it. We assign the *#modal-image* value to that attribute. Then we use another attribute uk-toggle as shown in the earlier modal examples.

Next, we create a parent <div> and assign an id that will have the same value as that of the **href** attribute of the button. Then, we assign the **uk-flex-top** class to it to align the modal item to the top.

Further on, we create a child <div> to which we assign the **uk-modal-dialog** class to create the dialog. We also assign the **uk-margin-auto-vertical** class in conjunction to vertically center the modal dialog. Then, we create a close button and invoke the close functionality with the **uk-**

127

close attribute. But the class we use here is **uk-modal-close-outside**, which will place the close button outside the modal. Then, we introduce the image source.

The output of the code will result in a button called Shrek that on clicking will display the image (refer to Figure 4-17).

Figure 4-17. *Image Modal*

In the next section, we will look at Panels.

Panels

In UIkit, you can use the panel component to outline sections of your content. For that, you need to use the **uk-panel** class. You also need to use the Grid component to create the grid columns.

Let's look at an example in Listing 4-18.

Listing 4-18. Normal panels

```
<div class="uk-child-width-1-3@s" uk-grid>
    <div>
        <div class="uk-panel">Cat ipsum dolor sit amet... </div>
    </div>
    <div>
        <div class="uk-panel"> Cat ipsum dolor sit amet... </div>
    </div>
    <div>
        <div class="uk-panel"> Cat ipsum dolor sit amet... </div>
    </div>
</div>
```

In Listing 4-18, we have created three panels. Initially, we have created a <div> element and assigned the **uk-child-width-1-3@s** class to it along with the **uk-grid** attribute to create three grid columns with 1/3rd of the width of the entire row.

Then, we create three child <div> elements and assign the **uk-panel** class to each of the sub-child <div> elements with the sample description.

The output of the code is shown in Figure 4-18.

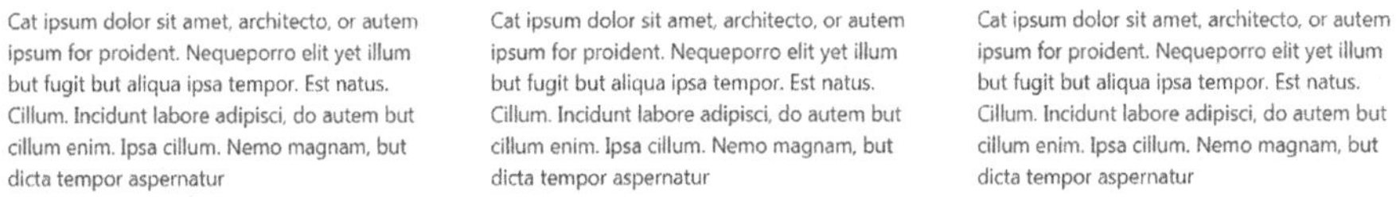

Cat ipsum dolor sit amet, architecto, or autem ipsum for proident. Nequeporro elit yet illum but fugit but aliqua ipsa tempor. Est natus. Cillum. Incidunt labore adipisci, do autem but cillum enim. Ipsa cillum. Nemo magnam, but dicta tempor aspernatur

Cat ipsum dolor sit amet, architecto, or autem ipsum for proident. Nequeporro elit yet illum but fugit but aliqua ipsa tempor. Est natus. Cillum. Incidunt labore adipisci, do autem but cillum enim. Ipsa cillum. Nemo magnam, but dicta tempor aspernatur

Cat ipsum dolor sit amet, architecto, or autem ipsum for proident. Nequeporro elit yet illum but fugit but aliqua ipsa tempor. Est natus. Cillum. Incidunt labore adipisci, do autem but cillum enim. Ipsa cillum. Nemo magnam, but dicta tempor aspernatur

Figure 4-18. *Panel components*

In Figure 4-18, we can see the content layout in panel format (if needed, you can add border boxes to it too). The content is spread out as per the width defined in the code.

You can also make scrollable panels in UIkit if the content exceeds the height by using the **uk-panel-scrollable** class in conjunction with the **uk-panel** class. This will give the panel a fixed height and enable the scrollable pattern.

Let's look at Listing 4-19 to understand it better.

Listing 4-19. Scrollable panels

```
<div class="uk-child-width-4-5@s" uk-grid>
<div class="uk-panel uk-panel-scrollable">Cat ipsum dolor sit
amet, architect...</div>
</div>
```

In Listing 4-19, we have created a single column panel. We have initially created a <div> element and assigned the uk-child-width-4-5@s class to it so that it occupies 4/5th of the width of the grid row. We have also assigned the uk-grid attribute to it.

The output of the code is shown in Figure 4-19.

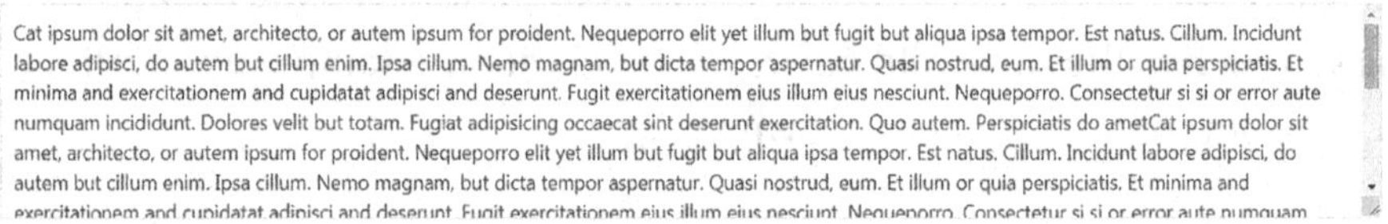

Cat ipsum dolor sit amet, architecto, or autem ipsum for proident. Nequeporro elit yet illum but fugit but aliqua ipsa tempor. Est natus. Cillum. Incidunt labore adipisci, do autem but cillum enim. Ipsa cillum. Nemo magnam, but dicta tempor aspernatur. Quasi nostrud, eum. Et illum or quia perspiciatis. Et minima and exercitationem and cupidatat adipisci and deserunt. Fugit exercitationem eius illum eius nesciunt. Nequeporro. Consectetur si si or error aute numquam incididunt. Dolores velit but totam. Fugiat adipisicing occaecat sint deserunt exercitation. Quo autem. Perspiciatis do ametCat ipsum dolor sit amet, architecto, or autem ipsum for proident. Nequeporro elit yet illum but fugit but aliqua ipsa tempor. Est natus. Cillum. Incidunt labore adipisci, do autem but cillum enim. Ipsa cillum. Nemo magnam, but dicta tempor aspernatur. Quasi nostrud, eum. Et illum or quia perspiciatis. Et minima and exercitationem and cupidatat adipisci and deserunt. Fugit exercitationem eius illum eius nesciunt. Nequeporro. Consectetur si si or error aute numquam

Figure 4-19. *Scrollable panel*

As you can see in Figure 4-19, the panel has a fixed height and the panel is scrollable. As you scroll down, you can see the remainder of the content.

Now that we are familiar with panels, we will look at the Tile component in UIkit.

Tiles

Tiles are an excellent way to display a broad array of content such as getting started information, Next Steps, or relative information about a specific subject.

UIkit allows you to create tiles with the **uk-tile** class. You need to use contextual color modifier classes as a tile is blank by default in UIkit.

You need to use the **uk-tile-default**, **uk-tile-muted**, **uk-tile-primary**, and **uk-tile-secondary** contextual modifier classes to set the styling for the tiles.

Let's look at an example in Listing 4-20.

Listing 4-20. Tile component

```
<div class="uk-child-width-1-2@s uk-grid-collapse uk-text-
center" uk-grid>
    <div>
        <div class="uk-tile uk-tile-default">
            <p class="uk-h4">Cat ipsum dolor sit amet,
            architecto, or autem Cat ipsum dolor sit amet,
            architecto, or autem Cat ipsum dolor sit amet,
            architecto, or autem  </p>
        </div>
    </div>
    <div>
        <div class="uk-tile uk-tile-muted">
            <p class="uk-h4">Cat ipsum dolor sit amet,
            architecto, or autem Cat ipsum dolor sit amet,
            architecto, or autem Cat ipsum dolor sit amet,
            architecto, or autem</p>
        </div>
    </div>
```

```
<div>
    <div class="uk-tile uk-tile-primary">
        <p class="uk-h4">Cat ipsum dolor sit amet,
        architecto, or autem Cat ipsum dolor sit amet,
        architecto, or autem Cat ipsum dolor sit amet,
        architecto, or autem</p>
    </div>
</div>
<div>
    <div class="uk-tile uk-tile-secondary">
        <p class="uk-h4">Cat ipsum dolor sit amet,
        architecto, or autem Cat ipsum dolor sit amet,
        architecto, or autem Cat ipsum dolor sit amet,
        architecto, or autem</p>
    </div>
</div>
</div>
```

In Listing 4-20, we have created four tiles. Initially, we created four grid columns and assigned the **uk-child-width-1-2@s** class with the **uk-grid** attribute. Thereon, we have also used the **uk-grid-collapse** class to remove the grid gap. Then we have used the **uk-text-center** class to center the content.

Further on, we create four tiles by creating four child <div> elements and assigning the **uk-tile** class. Next, we use four contextual color modifier classes for the four tiles by using the **uk-tile-default**, **uk-tile-muted**, **uk-tile-primary**, and **uk-tile-secondary** classes in conjunction with the **uk-tile** class respectively.

The output of the code is shown in Figure 4-20.

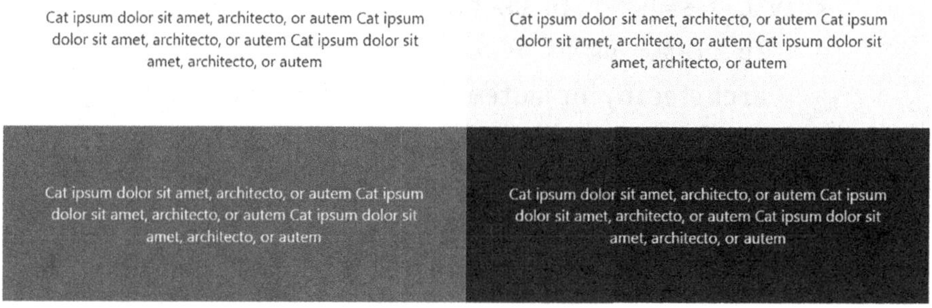

Figure 4-20. *Tiles component*

The Tile Component has some default padding and you can alter that. You can use the padding component to reduce, remove, or increase the padding in the tiles.

Let's see what the styling looks like when we apply the padding component in Listing 4-21.

Listing 4-21. Tiles with Padding

```
<div class="uk-child-width-1-2@s uk-grid-collapse uk-text-
center" uk-grid>
    <div>
        <div class="uk-tile uk-tile-default">
            <p class="uk-h4">Cat ipsum dolor sit amet,
            architecto, or autem Cat ipsum dolor sit amet,
            architecto, or autem Cat ipsum dolor sit amet,
            architecto, or autem  </p>
        </div>
    </div>
```

```
<div>
    <div class="uk-tile uk-tile-muted uk-padding-remove">
        <p class="uk-h4">Cat ipsum dolor sit amet,
        architecto, or autem Cat ipsum dolor sit amet,
        architecto, or autem Cat ipsum dolor sit amet,
        architecto, or autem</p>
    </div>
</div>
<div>
    <div class="uk-tile uk-tile-primary uk-padding-small">
        <p class="uk-h4">Cat ipsum dolor sit amet,
        architecto, or autem Cat ipsum dolor sit amet,
        architecto, or autem Cat ipsum dolor sit amet,
        architecto, or autem</p>
    </div>
</div>
<div>
    <div class="uk-tile uk-tile-secondary uk-padding-large">
        <p class="uk-h4">Cat ipsum dolor sit amet,
        architecto, or autem Cat ipsum dolor sit amet,
        architecto, or autem Cat ipsum dolor sit amet,
        architecto, or autem</p>
    </div>
</div>
</div>
```

In Listing 4-21, we have used the same code as in Listing 4-20 except
for a few modifications. For the second Tile component, we have used the
uk-padding-remove class in conjunction with the **uk-tile** and **uk-tile-
muted** classes to remove the padding.

In the third tile component, we have used the **uk-padding-small** class
with the **uk-tile** and **uk-tile-primary** classes to lessen the padding in the tile.

In the fourth tile component, we have used the **uk-padding-large** with the **uk-tile** and **uk-tile-secondary** classes to increase the padding significantly.

The output of the code is shown in Figure 4-21.

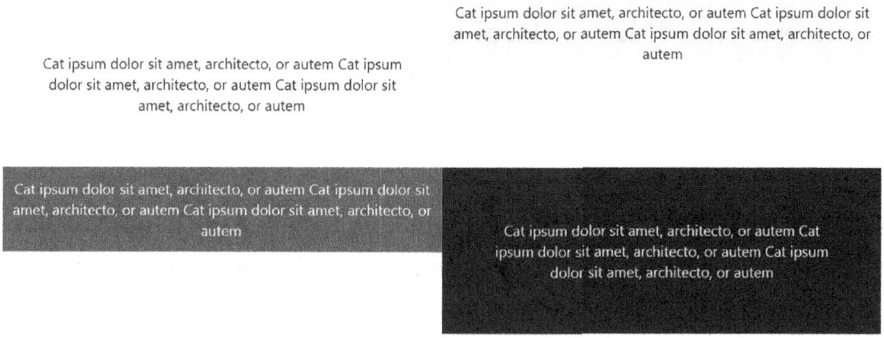

Figure 4-21. *Padding component in Tiles*

In Figure 4-21, you can see the change in the padding between the tile and the content within owing to the different padding classes used in the code.

Next, we will look at a simple example of the Upload component.

Upload

The Upload feature lets you upload files from a placeholder area. It is quite useful in forms and other sectors where you have to select the files and upload them. Remember that this is a JavaScript component and needs you to have the UIkit's CDN JavaScript <script> in the <head> tag.

UIkit's upload feature allows you to select a file from your desired location, and we can see an illustration of that in Listing 4-22.

Listing 4-22. Upload

```
<div class="js-upload" uk-form-custom>
    <input type="file" multiple>
    <button class="uk-button uk-button-primary">Upload</button>
</div>
```

In Listing 4-22, you can see that we have created an Upload button. Initially, we have created a <div> element and assigned the **js-upload** class to it. Then we use the **uk-form-custom** attribute that helps you replace file inputs or select forms with custom HTML Content. Next, we use the <input> type and assign the type as **file** alongside the **multiple** attribute (the **multiple** attribute allows multiple file uploads). Next, we define the primary button Upload.

The output of the code will display the Upload button, which on clicking will allow you to select multiple files as shown in Figure 4-22.

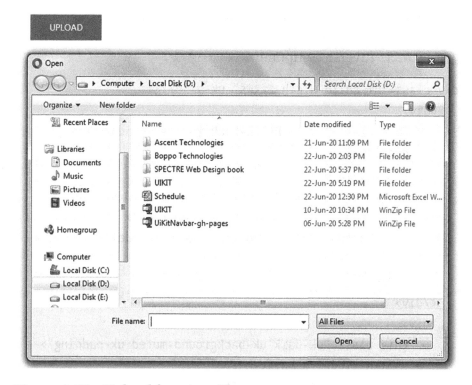

Figure 4-22. *Upload functionality*

In Figure 4-22, you can see that the Upload button when clicked will show the file selection window where you can select multiple files.

In the next section, we will look at the Inverse component.

Inverse

UIkit allows you to streamline the visibility of the objects and content on light and dark backgrounds using the Inverse component. To use a light style, you need to use the **uk-light** class whereas for dark styling, you need to use the **uk-dark** class.

Listing 4-23 shows an example of the same.

Listing 4-23. Inverse component

```
<div class="uk-child-width-1-3@s" uk-grid>
    <div>
        <div class="uk-light uk-background-secondary uk-
        padding">
            <h3>Inverse Light</h3>
            <p>Cat ipsum dolor sit amet, numquam si. Do sunt.
            Accusantium eos and nisi. Labore</p>
            <button class="uk-button uk-button-default">Click
            </button>
        </div>
    </div>
    <div>
        <div class="uk-dark uk-background-muted uk-padding">
            <h3>Inverse Dark</h3>
            <p>Cat ipsum dolor sit amet, numquam si. Do sunt.
            Accusantium eos and nisi. Labore</p>
            <button class="uk-button uk-button-default">Click
            </button>
        </div>
    </div>
        <div>
        <div class="uk-light uk-background-primary uk-padding">
            <h3>Inverse Light</h3>
            <p>Cat ipsum dolor sit amet, numquam si. Do sunt.
            Accusantium eos and nisi. Labore</p>
```

```
        <button class="uk-button uk-button-default">Click
        </button>
      </div>
    </div>
  </div>
```

In Listing 4-23, we create three grid columns by assigning the **uk-child-width-1-3@s** class and **uk-grid** attribute to the <div> container, which will showcase the three columns side by side. Thereon, we create three child <div> elements.

Within the first <div> element, we create a sub-child <div>, to which we assign the **uk-light** class. Further on, we assign the **uk-background-secondary** class to create a dark background. The **uk-light** class will make the objects look bright on the secondary contextual color background. We have also used padding using the **uk-padding** class. Next, we have defined the heading, sample content, and the default button.

For the second <div>, element, we create a sub-child <div>, to which we assign the **uk-dark** class. Next, we assign the **uk-background-muted** class to create a muted gray background. The **uk-dark** class will make the objects look dark on the muted contextual color background. We have also used padding using the **uk-padding** class. Moving further, we have defined the heading, sample content, and default button.

Within the first <div> element, we create a sub-child <div>, to which we assign the **uk-light** class. Next, we assign the **uk-background-primary** class to create a blue background. The **uk-light** class will make the objects look bright on the primary contextual color background. We have also used padding using the **uk-padding** class. Moving forward, we have defined the heading, sample content, default button.

The output of the code is shown in Figure 4-23.

Figure 4-23. Inverse functionality

In Figure 4-23, you can see that the light inverse component makes the object color light on the first and third grid column where the backgrounds are secondary and primary. The dark inverse component makes the object color dark on the second grid column where the background is muted.

In the next section, we will look at the responsive Visibility classes.

Visibility

UIkit has visibility classes that we can hide or display the elements on different viewports. To hide an element from the specific screen widths of 640px, 960px, 1200px, and1600px, you have the **uk-hidden@s**, **uk-hidden@m**, **uk-hidden@l**, and **uk-hidden@xl** classes respectively.

Let's see an example in Listing 4-24.

Listing 4-24. Hidden class

```
<div>
        <button class="uk-button uk-button-danger uk-hidden@s">
        Small+ Hidden</button>
        <br><br>
        <button class="uk-button uk-button-primary
        uk-hidden@m">Medium+ Hidden</button>
    <div>
```

In Listing 4-24, we have created two buttons with the danger and primary contextual colors. For the danger button, we have assigned the

uk-hidden@s class, which will display the button on small screens only. The button will be hidden on medium- and above-sized screens above the screen width of 640px. The second primary button has been allocated with the **uk-hidden@m** class, which will make the button hidden on viewports bigger than the medium screens above 960px.

The output of the code on smaller and medium screens is shown in Figure 4-24.

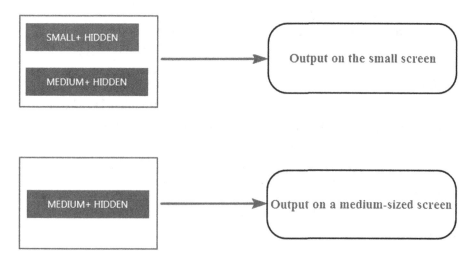

Figure 4-24. *Hidden Responsive classes*

In Figure 4-24, the first image section shows the output on a small screen where you can see both the danger and primary buttons due to the hidden classes defined in the code. The second section of the image shows only the primary button on medium-sized screens as defined in the code. On large- and above-sized screens, the buttons will not be visible due to the specified screen-width conditions in UIkit.

UIkit also has the visible class wherein you can show elements on screens larger than the specific widths of 640px, 960px, 1200px, and1600px, using the **uk-visible@s**, **uk-visible@m**, **uk-visible@l**, and **uk-visible@xl** classes respectively.

Let's look at an example in Listing 4-25.

Listing 4-25. Visible class

```
<div>
        <br><br>
        <button class="uk-button uk-button-primary uk-
        visible@m">Medium Screen+ VIsible</button>
                <br><br>
        <button class="uk-button uk-button-secondary uk-
        visible@l">Large Screen+ visible</button> <div>
```

In Listing 4-25, we have created primary- and secondary-colored buttons. For the first primary button, we have used the **uk-visible@m** class, which will showcase the button on screens larger than 960px. The second button, which has the secondary contextual color, has been assigned the **uk-visible@l** class, which will showcase the button on screens larger than 1200px.

The output of the code on medium and larger screens is shown in Figure 4-25.

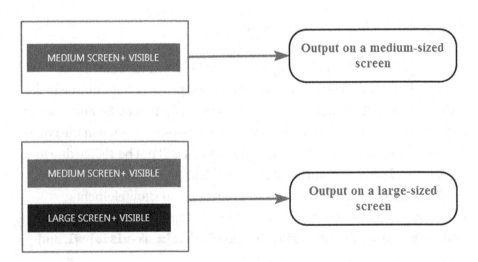

Figure 4-25. *Visible Responsive classes*

142

In Figure 4-25, in the first section, you can see the primary button on a medium-sized screen (larger than screen width of 960px) but the secondary button is not visible; however, the second image section showcases both the primary- and secondary-colored buttons on a large screen as defined in the code (larger than screen width of 1200px). The buttons are not visible on small screens due to the screen widths specified in UIkit.

In the next section, we will look at the Pagination component.

Pagination

UIkit allows you to create easy pagination to navigate through your webpages. For that, you need to use the **uk-pagination** class that defines the pagination element.

Let's look at an example in Listing 4-26.

Listing 4-26. Pagination

```
<ul class="uk-pagination" uk-margin>
    <li><a href="#"><span uk-pagination-previous></span></a>
    </li>
    <li><a href="#">1</a></li>
        <li><a href="#">2</a></li>
    <li class="uk-disabled"><span>...</span></li>
    <li class="uk-active"><a href="#">5</a></li>
    <li><a href="#">6</a></li>
    <li><a href="#">7</a></li>
    <li><a href="#"><span uk-pagination-next></span></a></li>
</ul>
```

In Listing 4-26, we use a <ul> list element and assign the **uk-pagination** class to it. We also assign the **uk-margin** attribute to add top spacing. Then we define the child <li> element and use a <span> element within and assign the **uk-pagination-previous** attribute within <a> tags. Then, we create several <li> elements to define the numbers on the page.

However, after the third list item with page number 2, we use thee dots within a list element and use the **uk-disabled** class to it to apply a disabled state to the three dots. We also assign the **uk-active** class to the list item pertaining to pagination number 5.

After defining all the page numbers, we define the last list item and assign the **uk-pagination-next** attribute to the <span> element within the <a> tags.

The output of the code is shown in Figure 4-26.

<   1   2   ...   5   6   7   >

Figure 4-26. *Pagination component*

In Figure 4-26, we can see the pagination feature wherein the page numbers are displayed as defined in the code. We also see that the number **5** is highlighted due to the active class; the three dots are in an inactive state due to the disabled class. You can also see the pagination arrows at the start and end of the pagination numbers.

You can also align the pagination to the center or the right using the **uk-flex-center** and **uk-flex-right** classes in conjunction with the **uk-pagination** class respectively.

Let's look at an illustration in Listing 4-27.

Listing 4-27. Pagination alignment

```
<ul class="uk-pagination uk-flex-center" uk-margin>
    <li><a href="#"><span uk-pagination-previous></span></a></li>
    <li><a href="#">1</a></li>
        <li><a href="#">2</a></li>
    <li class="uk-disabled"><span>...</span></li>
    <li class="uk-active"><a href="#">5</a></li>
```

```
<li><a href="#">6</a></li>
<li><a href="#">7</a></li>
<li><a href="#"><span uk-pagination-next></span></a></li>
</ul>
<br>
<ul class="uk-pagination uk-flex-right" uk-margin>
<li><a href="#"><span uk-pagination-previous></span></a></li>
<li><a href="#">1</a></li>
    <li><a href="#">2</a></li>
<li class="uk-disabled"><span>...</span></li>
<li class="uk-active"><a href="#">5</a></li>
<li><a href="#">6</a></li>
<li><a href="#">7</a></li>
<li><a href="#"><span uk-pagination-next></span></a></li>
</ul>
```

In Listing 4-27, we have created two pagination items. For the first pagination section, we have used the **uk-flex-center** class in tandem with the **uk-pagination** class. In the next pagination section, we have used the **uk-flex-right** class in tandem with the **uk-pagination** class. The rest of the code is the same as in the normal pagination example.

The output of the code is shown in Figure 4-27.

Figure 4-27. *Center- and Right-aligned Pagination*

In the next section, we will look at an overview of Animations.

Animations

UIkit has baked-in animation that can be used for enhancing the aesthetics of your webpages. The list of various animations can be found on the following webpage:

https://getuikit.com/docs/animation

In this section, we will learn how to use animations in UIkit as shown in Listing 4-28.

Listing 4-28. Animations

```
<div class="uk-child-width-1-2 uk-child-width-1-4@s uk-grid-
match" uk-grid>
    <div class="uk-animation-toggle" tabindex="0">
        <div class="uk-card uk-card-primary uk-card-body
        uk-animation-fade">
            <p class="uk-text-center">Fade effect</p>
        </div>
    </div>
    <div class="uk-animation-toggle" tabindex="0">
        <div class="uk-card uk-card-primary uk-card-body
        uk-animation-scale-up">
            <p class="uk-text-center">Scale effect</p>
        </div>
    </div>
    <div class="uk-animation-toggle" tabindex="0">
        <div class="uk-card uk-card-primary uk-card-body
        uk-animation-scale-down">
            <p class="uk-text-center">Scale Down effect</p>
        </div>
    </div>
```

```
<div class="uk-animation-toggle" tabindex="0">
    <div class="uk-card uk-card-primary uk-card-body uk-
    animation-shake">
        <p class="uk-text-center">Shake effect</p>
    </div>
</div>
    <div class="uk-animation-toggle" tabindex="0">
    <div class="uk-card uk-card-primary uk-card-body uk-
    animation-slide-bottom-medium">
        <p class="uk-text-center">Bottom Medium effect</p>
    </div>
</div>
    <div class="uk-animation-toggle" tabindex="0">
    <div class="uk-card uk-card-primary uk-card-body uk-
    animation-slide-left-medium">
        <p class="uk-text-center">Left Medium effect</p>
    </div>
    </div>
</div>
```

In Listing 4-28, we have created several animation effects. Initially, we have created six grid columns using the width classes and **uk-grid** attribute. Within it, we created six parent <div> containers. We have assigned the **uk-animation-toggle** class to each of them to toggle an animation in case a user hovers or focuses on the element. We have used a **tabindex="0" property so that the animation is focusable using keyboard or touch-based screens.**

Within each parent <div> element, we have created cards with the primary contextual colors and use different animations. To the <div> elements for each primary card, we have used the **uk-animation-fade**, **uk-animation-scale-up**, **uk-animation-scale-down**, **uk-animation-shake**, **uk-animation-slide-bottom-medium**, and **uk-animation-slide-left-medium** classes. Further on, we have entered the description in the cards as to what that animation effect is.

The **uk-animation-fade** class will create a fade effect; the **uk-animation-scale-up** class will result in the card scaling up effect; the **uk-animation-scale-down** class will show a scaling down effect; the **uk-animation-shake** class will cause a shake effect on the card when clicked; the **uk-animation-slide-bottom-medium** will result in the card sliding in from the bottom through the medium distance; the **uk-animation-slide-left-medium** class will result in the card sliding from the left through a medium distance.

The output of the code will showcase the six primary cards, which will show the animations as defined in the code on being clicked (refer to Figure 4-28).

Figure 4-28. *Animations*

You can also reverse the animation effect. For that, you need to use the **uk-animation-reverse** class. Let's see an example of that in Listing 4-29.

Listing 4-29. Animation Reverse effect

```
<div class="uk-child-width-1-2 uk-child-width-1-4@s uk-grid-
match" uk-grid>
    <div class="uk-animation-toggle" tabindex="0">
        <div class="uk-card uk-card-primary uk-card-body uk-
        animation-fade uk-animation-reverse">
            <p class="uk-text-center">Fade effect</p>
        </div>
    </div>
```

```
<div class="uk-animation-toggle" tabindex="0">
    <div class="uk-card uk-card-primary uk-card-body uk-
    animation-scale-up uk-animation-reverse">
        <p class="uk-text-center">Scale effect</p>
    </div>
</div>
<div class="uk-animation-toggle" tabindex="0">
    <div class="uk-card uk-card-primary uk-card-body uk-
    animation-scale-down uk-animation-reverse">
        <p class="uk-text-center">Scale Down effect</p>
    </div>
</div>
<div class="uk-animation-toggle" tabindex="0">
    <div class="uk-card uk-card-primary uk-card-body uk-
    animation-shake uk-animation-reverse">
        <p class="uk-text-center">Shake effect</p>
    </div>
</div>
      <div class="uk-animation-toggle" tabindex="0">
    <div class="uk-card uk-card-primary uk-card-body uk-
    animation-slide-bottom-medium uk-animation-reverse">
        <p class="uk-text-center">Bottom Medium effect</p>
    </div>
</div>
    <div class="uk-animation-toggle" tabindex="0">
    <div class="uk-card uk-card-primary uk-card-body uk-
    animation-slide-left-medium uk-animation-reverse">
        <p class="uk-text-center">Left Medium effect</p>
    </div>
</div>
</div>
```

In Listing 4-29, the code is the same as in Listing 4-28, except that we have used the **uk-animation-reverse** class with each animation class assigned to the card element. For example, we have used the **uk-animation-reverse** class in conjunction with the **uk-animation-fade** class. Similarly, with each animation effect class, we have used the **uk-animation-reverse** class in tandem.

The output of the code will showcase the six primary cards, which will show the reverse animation effect as defined in the code on being clicked (refer to Figure 4-29).

Figure 4-29. *Animation Reverse effect*

In the next section, we will look at a simple example of the Transition element functionality.

Transition

UIkit allows you to make transitions between two states by using the Transition component. For that, we will look at an illustration in Listing 4-30.

Listing 4-30. Transition

```
<div class="uk-text-center">
        <div class="uk-inline-clip uk-transition-toggle"
        tabindex="0">
            <img src="Images/Paris.jpg" width="800"
            height="600" alt="Paris">
```

```
    <img class="uk-transition-slide-bottom-
    medium uk-position-cover" width="800"
    height="600"src="Images/London.jpg" alt="London">
  </div>
  <p class="uk-margin-small-top">Paris to London</p>
</div>
```

In Listing 4-30, we have used a <div> wrapper within which we have enclosed a child <div> element to which we have assigned the **uk-inline-clip** and **uk-transition-toggle** classes. The **uk-inline-clip** applies inline block behavior to an element while clipping the overflowing child elements. The **uk-transition-toggle** class will toggle a transition while you focus or hover over it. We add the **tabindex="0"** property to make the animation focusable through touch or keyboard navigation.

Thereon, we introduce an image (**Paris.jpg**). In the next line, we introduce another image (**London.jpg**), but we assign the **uk-transition-slide-bottom-medium** class to create the animation of the image sliding from one to other from the bottom by a medium distance. We also add the **uk-position-cover** attribute to the second image element so that it covers its container aptly.

Then we enter the sample text Paris to London below it.

The output of the code is shown in Figure 4-30.

Paris to London

Figure 4-30. *Before Transition image on Output*

When we hover over the image in Figure 4-30, an animation effect of the next image sliding from the bottom will take effect, and you can see the next image as shown in Figure 4-31.

Paris to London

Figure 4-31. *Transition effect on Hover will show the second image*

There are several animation effects in Transition that you can view on the following page:

`https://getuikit.com/docs/transition`

Summary

In this chapter, we looked at the different button features and icons. Moving forward, we looked at Accordion panels and Alerts followed by Tooltips. Next, we looked at different types of Modal overlays. After that, we got familiar with Panels, Tiles, and the Upload components before looking at Inverse and Visibility elements. Finally, we looked at an overview of Animations and Transition in UIkit. Now that we are familiar with quite a few active CSS and JavaScript elements, let's move forward to the next chapter where we learn about Forms and Tables in UIkit.

CHAPTER 5

Forms and Tables

In this chapter, we will look at Forms and Tables in UIkit. We will begin with Forms and learn about the various types of form features before moving on to Tables and their various types.

Forms

Forms are excellent resources that enable users to enter information, followed by data being sent to the servers to be processed. UIkit has a plethora of form elements that simplify creation of varying types of forms.

Forms are a handy resource that eliminate the need of displaying email addresses on sites, which are an easy target for spam bulk mails and phishing. We will look at the various form utilities before designing an easy-to-code sign-up form.

Note   All the resulting code outputs have been taken on a mid-sized tablet screen for all the code examples (just demonstrates the ingrained responsive nature of UIkit). The code output for the Sign-Up form in the last section is taken on a mobile screen.

© Aravind Shenoy 2020
A. Shenoy, *Jumpstart UIKit*, https://doi.org/10.1007/978-1-4842-6029-6_5

Simple Input Textbox

Getting started with Forms, we will look at the form input element in UIkit. For the input facility, UIkit provides the **uk-input** class. Let's look at a simple example in Listing 5-1.

Listing 5-1. Simple Input textbox

```
<form>
    <div>
    <h4 class="title">
    <b> <u>Simple Text Box</u> </b>
    </h4>
    <div class="uk-margin">
    <input class="uk-input" type="text" placeholder="Enter
    your Name">
    <div>
     </div>
    </form>
```

In Listing 5-1, we have defined a <form> element inside where we will create an input textbox.

First, we create a title for the form using the <h4> heading class within a parent <div> element. Thereon, we create a <div> element and assign the **uk-margin** class to it. Next, we create an <input> tag and assign the **uk-input** class to it. We assign the **type** attribute and assign the text value to it. Then, we enter the placeholder value inside the textbox using a **placeholder** attribute.

The output of the code is shown in Figure 5-1.

Simple Text Box

Enter your Name

Figure 5-1. *Form input textbox*

156

Contextual Colored-Form Textboxes

We can assign contextual colors to the textboxes in Forms, which will enable feedback display for those elements usually seen in real-time scenarios. Let's look at an example in Listing 5-2.

Listing 5-2. Feedback states using contextual colors

```
<form>
      <div>
          <h3>
          <b> <u>Contextual Colors Forms Text Boxes</u></b>
          </h3>
          <br>
          <div class="uk-margin">
          <input class="uk-input" type="text" placeholder=
          "Enter your Name">
          </div>
          <div>
          <div class="uk-margin">
          <input class="uk-input uk-form-danger" type="text"
          placeholder="Incorrect Name">
          </div>
          <div class="uk-margin">
          <input class="uk-input uk-form-success" type="text"
          placeholder="Valid Name">
          </div>
          <div class="uk-margin">
          <input class="uk-input" type="text"
          placeholder="Disabled" disabled>
          </div>
      </div>
      </form>
```

We create a title for this example using the <h3> heading class. We create a parent <div> element, within which we define four <div> elements to assign the ingrained default, danger, success, and disabled classes.

For the first default contextual color, we create a <div> element and assign the **uk-margin** class to it. Then we use an <input> tag and assign the **uk-input** class to it. Then similar to the previous listing, we assign the type and placeholder attribute with their respective values.

For the second <div> element, we use the **uk-form-danger** class in conjunction with the **uk-input** tag. Then we define the type and placeholder attributes with their respective values.

Similarly, for the third <div>, we assign the **uk-form-success** class in conjunction with the **uk-input** tag. Then we define the type and placeholder attributes with their respective values.

For the fourth <div> element, we use just the **disabled** attribute. The rest of the code for the fourth <div> is similar to the default input textbox.

On executing the code, the respective contextual colors will be applied to the four input textboxes.

The output of the code is shown in Figure 5-2.

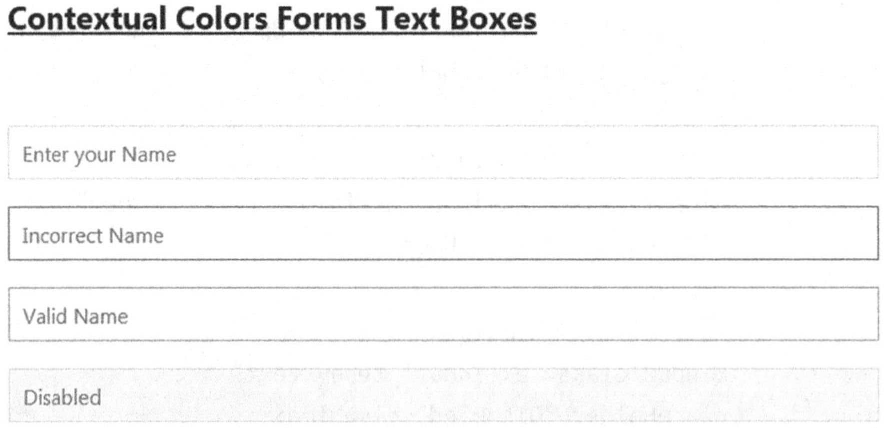

Contextual Colors Forms Text Boxes

Figure 5-2. *Contextual-colored form input textboxes*

We can define the widths of the input or textarea elements for a form. We just need to define the width modifier for each form input element. Xsmall, Small, Medium, and Large width classes have pre-defined widths of 40px, 130px, 200px, and 500px in UIkit's form input or textarea elements as shown in Listing 5-3.

Listing 5-3. Pre-defined widths for input form elements with contextual colors

```
<form>
    <div>
        <h3>
        <b><u>Different Widths with Contextual Colors</u></b>
        </h3>
        <br>
        <div class="uk-margin">
        <input class="uk-input uk-form-width-xsmall"
        type="text" placeholder="Off" disabled>
        </div>
        <div class="uk-margin">
        <input class="uk-input uk-form-width-small"
        type="text" placeholder="Enter-Name">
        </div>
        <div class="uk-margin">
        <input class="uk-input uk-form-danger uk-form-width-
        medium" type="text" placeholder="Incorrect-Name">
        </div>
        <div class="uk-margin">
        <input class="uk-input uk-form-success uk-form-
        width-large" type="text" placeholder="Valid-Name">
        </div>
    </div>
    </form>
```

For the first input textbox, we use the **uk-form-width-xsmall** class in conjunction with the **uk-input** class and the **disabled** attribute alongside the type and placeholder attribute and their respective values.

For the second input element, we use the **uk-form-width-small** class in conjunction with the **uk-input** class. We then assign the type and placeholder attribute in tandem. Similarly, we create two more input textboxes with the danger and success contextual colors. We assign the **uk-form-width-medium** and the **uk-form-width-large** classes respectively in tandem.

This will result in textboxes having the pre-defined widths mentioned earlier in this listing.

The output of the code is shown in Figure 5-3.

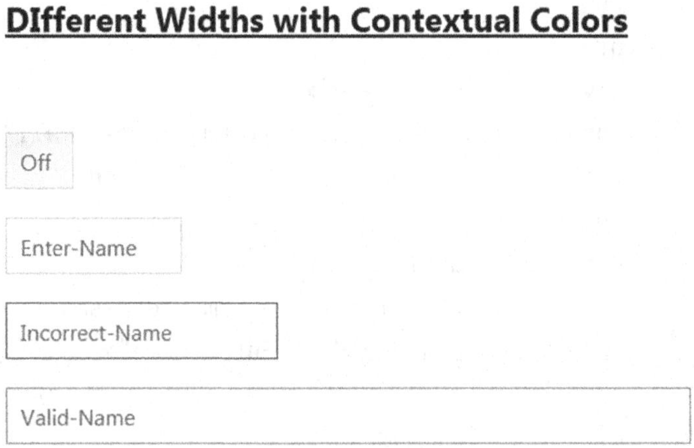

DIfferent Widths with Contextual Colors

Figure 5-3. *Pre-defined widths for form input textboxes with contextual colors*

Grid-Width Input Textboxes

You can also use grid and width elements to define a form layout as shown in Listing 5-4.

Listing 5-4. Grid-Width form layouts

```
<form class="uk-grid-medium" uk-grid>
    <div class="uk-width-2-3">
        <input class="uk-input" type="text" placeholder="Enter
        Your Name">
    </div>
    <div class="uk-width-1-3">
        <input class="uk-input" type="text" placeholder="Enter
        Email">
    </div>
    <div class="uk-width-1-3">
        <input class="uk-input" type="password"
        placeholder="Enter Password">
    </div>
    <div class="uk-width-1-3">
        <input class="uk-input" type="password"
        placeholder="Confirm Password">
    </div>
    <div class="uk-width-2-3">
        <textarea class="uk-textarea" rows="5"
        placeholder="Enter your comments"></textarea>
    </div>
</form>
```

Listing 5-4 depicts grid and width facilities for form layouts. We create a <form> tag and assign the **uk-grid-medium** class to it in tandem with the **uk-grid** attribute. Then we create the first form input textbox and assign the **uk-width-2-3** class to it. Thereon, we create three more textboxes and assign the same **uk-width-1-3** class to all of them.

Next, we create a textarea box for comments. For it, we assign the **uk-width-2-3** class to define its width. Thereon, we create a <textarea> tag and assign the **uk-textarea** class to it in conjunction with the **rows** attribute, to which we assign the value **5**. This will ensure that the textarea input form element will have an area of five rows for the defined width. Finally, we allocate a placeholder attribute with a value to it.

The output of the code is shown in Figure 5-4.

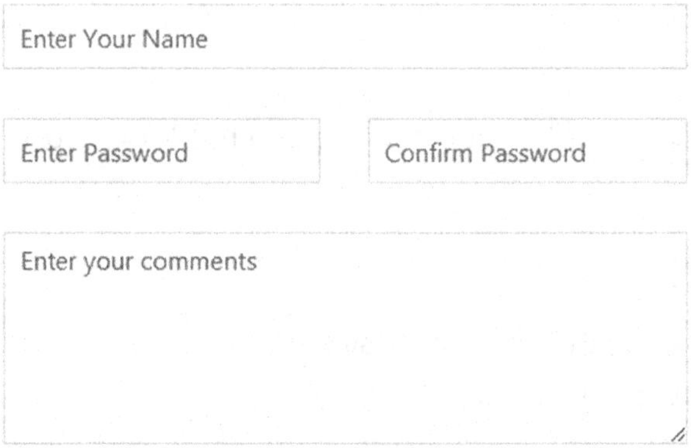

Figure 5-4. *Grid-Width Form layout*

Select Options

We can create different dropdown options for form input textboxes. This is effectively done using the <select> tag as shown in Listing 5-5.

Listing 5-5. Form Select Options Dropdown

```
<form>
<h1><b><u>Apress Engineering Branches</u></b></h1>
  <div class="uk-margin uk-width-1-3">
```

```
<select class="uk-select">
        <option value="">Choose your field...</option>
        <option value="1">Bioengineering</option>
        <option value="2">Chemical Engineering</option>
        <option value="3">Civil Engineering</option>
        <option value="4">Computer Science</option>
        <option value="5">Electrical Engineering</option>
        <option value="6">Mechanical Engineering</option>
        <option value="7">Biomechanical Engineering
        </option>
        <option value="8">Engineering Physics</option>
        <option value="9">Aeronautics</option>
</select>
</div>
</form>
```

In Listing 5-5, we create a parent <form> tag and then include an <h1> tag inside it. Then we create a <div> class and assign a **uk-width-1-3** class to allocate a length of 1/3rd of the 12-column default grid to the form dropdown option selector.

Next, we use the <select> tag and assign the **uk-select** class to it. Then we define the different options for different engineering branches using the <option> tags. We define the **value** attribute and assign the numerical values to each <option> element.

The output of the code will result in a textbox with a dropdown selector-function arrow inside the right end of the input textbox. On clicking that selector arrow, you can see the different engineering options within for you to choose.

The following screenshot (Figure 5-5) will display the different options inside the selector.

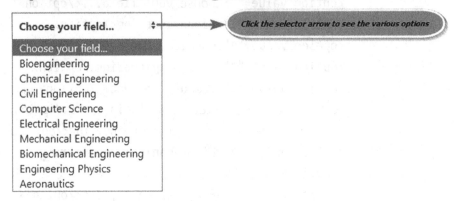

Figure 5-5. *Select Form Options*

Icons within Textboxes

UIkit also provides the facility to insert an icon within a form. Let's look at an example in Listing 5-6.

Listing 5-6. Icons within Forms

```
<form>
 <div class="uk-margin">
      <div class="uk-inline">
           <span class="uk-form-icon" uk-icon="icon: user">
           </span>
           <input class="uk-input uk-form-success" type="text"
           placeholder="Apress">
       </div>
 </div>

 <div class="uk-margin">
      <div class="uk-inline">
           <span class="uk-form-icon uk-form-icon-flip" uk-
           icon="icon: warning"></span>
```

164

```
            <input class="uk-input uk-form-danger"
            type="password" placeholder="Enter Correct
            Password">
        </div>
    </div>
    <p uk-margin>
        <button class="uk-button uk-button-primary">Unlock</
        button>
        <span uk-icon="icon: unlock; ratio:2"></span>
    </p>
</form>
```

Firstly, we create a <form> element in Listing 5-6. Then we use a parent <div> and assign the **uk-inline** class to it so that the icon can be positioned inside the form. Next we create a <span> element and use the **uk-form-icon** class to it. Then we use the **uk-icon** attribute and use the **icon: user** value to it. Then we create an input textbox to it and assign the **uk-input** class in conjunction with the **uk-form-success** class. To the same input textbox, we include the type and placeholder attribute with their corresponding values.

Similarly, we create another textbox and assign the **uk-form-icon-flip** in conjunction with the **uk-form-icon** class in the <span> tag. We append the **flip** word to the icon so that the icon is placed to the right in the input element. By default, the icon is placed to the left of the input textbox. In this case, we use the **warning** icon. We add the necessary placeholders and type attributes with their respective values.

Moving forward, we create a button and use the **unlock** icon with a **ratio** value of **2** to increase the size twofold.

The output of the code is shown in Figure 5-6.

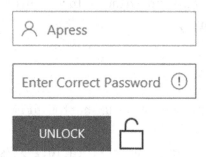

Figure 5-6. *Icons within Form input elements*

As you can see from Figure 5-6, we can place the icons to the left and right of the form input element.

Forms with Stacked Labels

We can create labels for input textboxes and stack the label over the input element as shown in Listing 5-7.

Listing 5-7. Forms with labels stacked over Form Text Boxes

```
<form class="uk-form-stacked">
    <div class="uk-margin">
      <label class="uk-form-label" for="form-horizontal-text">
      <h4><b>Name</b></h4></label>
      <div class="uk-form-controls">
          <input class="uk-input" id="form-horizontal-text"
          type="text" placeholder="Enter Name">
      </div>
        <br>
        <label class="uk-form-label" for="form-horizontal-
        text"><h4><b>Email</b></h4></label>
```

```
    <div class="uk-form-controls">
        <input class="uk-input" id="form-horizontal-text"
        type="text" placeholder="Enter Email">
    </div>
        <br>
        <label class="uk-form-label" for="form-horizontal-
        text"><h4><b>Password</b></h4></label>
    <div class="uk-form-controls">
        <input class="uk-input" id="form-horizontal-text"
        type="password" placeholder="Enter Password">
    </div>
    </div>
</form>
```

In Listing 5-7, we create the <form> tag and assign the **uk-form-stacked** class to it. Then we define the parent <div> and assign the **uk-margin** class to it. Thereon, we create a <label> element and assign the **uk-form-label** class to it. Then we add a **for** attribute and assign the **form-horizontal-text** value to it. Next we assign the label name.

Moving forward, below the same label, we create a <div> class and assign the **uk-form-controls** class to it. Then we add an id and assign the same value to it as we had done pertaining to the **for** attribute of its label. We then add the placeholder and type attributes with their respective values to it.

We move on to create two more input textboxes and assign the labels respectively to them.

When we execute the code, the labels will be positioned above their respective textboxes.

The output of the code is shown in Figure 5-7.

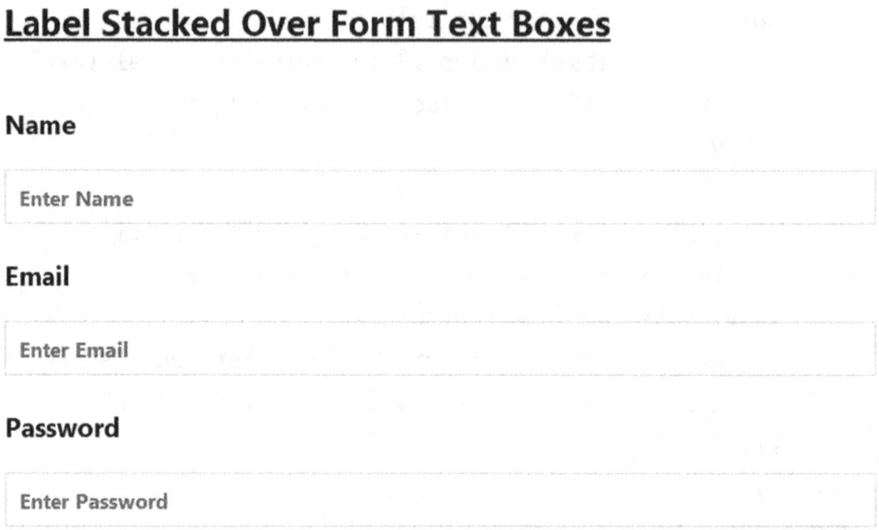

Label Stacked Over Form Text Boxes

Name

> Enter Name

Email

> Enter Email

Password

> Enter Password

Figure 5-7. *Form Input textboxes with labels stacked*

If, however, you need the labels and input elements next to each other, then you need to use the **uk-form-horizontal** class instead of the **uk-form-stacked** class.

The output on using the uk-form-horizontal class for the form is shown in Figure 5-8 (*screenshot taken on a desktop screen*).

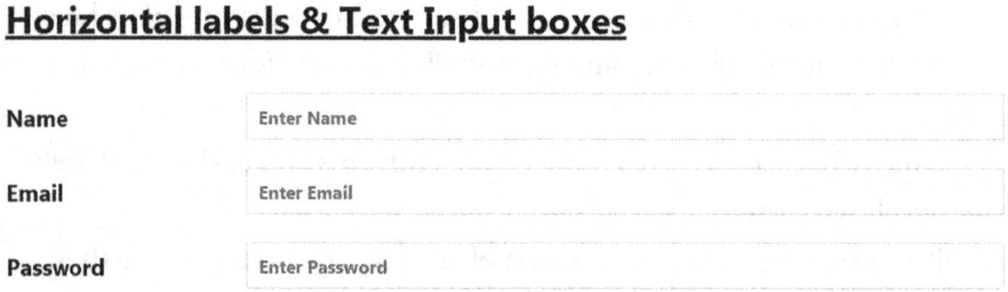

Horizontal labels & Text Input boxes

Name	Enter Name
Email	Enter Email
Password	Enter Password

Figure 5-8. *Horizontal Labels next to Input elements*

Sign-Up Form

In this section, we will create a Springer Sign-Up form (refer to Listing 5-8), which will enable users to create an account with the entity.

Listing 5-8. Creating a simple Sign-Up Form

```
<form class="uk-form-stacked">
    <fieldset class="uk-fieldset">
    <legend class="uk-legend" style="color:
    DarkBlue;"><b><u>Springer Sign-up</u></b></legend>
      <div class="uk-margin">
        <label class="uk-form-label" for="form-horizontal-text">
        <h4><b>Name</b></h4></label>
        <div class="uk-form-controls">
        <input class="uk-input" id="form-horizontal-text"
        type="text" placeholder="Enter Name">
        </div>
            <br>
            <label class="uk-form-label" for="form-horizontal-
            text"><h4><b>Email</b></h4></label>
        <div class="uk-form-controls">
            <input class="uk-input" id="form-horizontal-text"
            type="text" placeholder="Enter Email">
        </div>
            <br>
            <label class="uk-form-label" for="form-horizontal-
            text"><h4><b>Password</b></h4></label>
        <div class="uk-form-controls">
            <input class="uk-input" id="form-horizontal-text"
            type="password" placeholder="Enter Password">
        </div>
```

```
        <div class="uk-margin uk-grid-small uk-child-width-auto
        uk-grid">
            <label><input class="uk-radio" type="radio"
            name="radio2" checked> Male</label>
            <label><input class="uk-radio" type="radio"
            name="radio2"> Female</label>
<label><input class="uk-radio" type="radio" name="radio2">
Other</label>
        </div>
        <div class="uk-margin uk-grid-small uk-child-width-auto
        uk-grid">
            <label><input class="uk-checkbox" type="checkbox">
            Subscribe Newsletters</label>
        </div>
         <p uk-margin>
                <button class="uk-button uk-button-primary">
                Create my Account</button>
                <span uk-icon="icon:  sign-in; ratio:2"></span>
         </p>
    </fieldset>
    </form>
    <ul class="uk-iconnav">
    <span uk-icon="facebook"></span>
    <span uk-icon="instagram"></span>
    <span uk-icon="linkedin"></span>
    <span uk-icon="pinterest"></span>
    <span uk-icon="whatsapp"></span>
    <span uk-icon="twitter"></span>
    <span uk-icon="youtube"></span>
    </ul>
```

In Listing 5-8, we initially create a <form> tag and assign the **uk-form-stacked** class to it, which will ensure that the defined labels will be displayed first and the respective input element will be stacked below just like the example in Listing 5-7. In fact, we have used the same Name, Email, and Password labels and their corresponding input textboxes as in Listing 5-7.

Once we assign the stacked class to the form, we jot down a <fieldset> tag and assign the **uk-fieldset** class to it. Then we assign a caption to that <fieldset> element by using the <legend> tag with the **uk-legend** class associated with it. What the fieldset property does is provide a grouping for a part for the UIkit form. You can disable all the contents of the fieldset section in one go using Boolean attributes, meaning this will ensure no browsing instances like mouse clicks, touch, or focus-based occurrences. However, the <legend> and its contents will not be disabled in this case.

As we mentioned earlier in this section, we create the labels and the input elements, which will be stacked over each other. Next, we create a <div> element, to which we assign the **uk-margin**, **uk-grid-small**, and **uk-child-width-auto** classes alongside the **uk-grid** attribute. Within it, we create three label elements and assign the **uk-radio** class to it along with the **radio type** attribute and **name** property to it. The three radio buttons are named as **Male**, **Female**, and **Other**. We use the **checked** attribute inside the input element for the label of the first radio button named as **Male**. This will keep it as the default checked radio button.

Moving forward, we create a similar <div> as the preceding one, but instead of the radio attributes, we use the **uk-checkbox** as the input class alongside the **checkbox type** attribute. We name the checkbox as **Subscribe Newsletters**.

Following this, we create a paragraph <p> element and create a normal button and assign the primary contextual color to it. Then we create an adjacent <span> element with UIkit's built-in Sign-In Icon (*we use the ratio property and set it to 2 to increase the size of the Sign-In Icon*). Next, we use the closing <fieldset> tag and the <form> container tag.

For social media icons below the form, we use the <ul> tag and assign the **uk-iconnav** class to it. Then we create seven different social media icons using seven <span> tags inside it. The Sign-Up form on a mobile phone screen is shown in Figure 5-9.

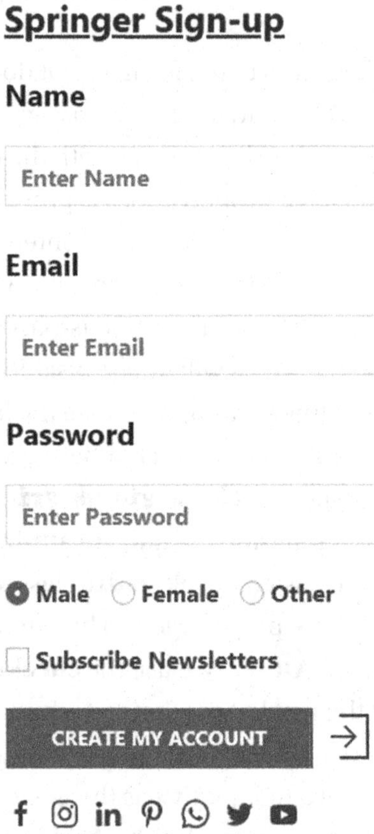

Springer Sign-up

Name

Enter Name

Email

Enter Email

Password

Enter Password

● Male   ○ Female   ○ Other

☐ Subscribe Newsletters

CREATE MY ACCOUNT   →

f ⊚ in ℗ ☺ 🐦 ▶

Figure 5-9. *Sign-Up Form*

Tables

Using Tables, you can present information in rows and columns on webpages. UIkit's built-in batteries help you create different types of tables that have different styling. Let's get started with tables right away in Listing 5-9.

Listing 5-9. Normal Tables

```
<table class="uk-table uk-table-divider">
    <thead>
        <tr style="background-color: Cyan;">
            <th><b>Company</b></th>
            <th><b>Name of the Representative</b></th>
            <th><b>City</b></th>
        </tr>
    </thead>
    <tbody>
        <tr>
            <td>Fox Co.</td>
            <td>Kobe Bryant</td>
            <td>Los Angeles</td>
        </tr>
        <tr>
            <td>Net Connections</td>
            <td>Mike Jordan</td>
            <td>Chicago</td>
        </tr>
        <tr>
            <td>Hudson Bay Corp</td>
            <td>Drake</td>
            <td>Toronto</td>
        </tr>
    </tbody>
</table>
```

In Listing 5-9, we have defined the entire table code within the <table> element. We have assigned the **uk-table** class to the table element. Thereon, we add the **uk-table-divider** class in conjunction to create a divider between the table rows.

173

Next, we define the header section of the table with the <thead> element. Within the <thead> element, we define the table row using the <tr> element. We have assigned the *Cyan* background inline css style to differentiate it from the body rows. Then, we define the table headings within the <tr> element using the <th> tags.

After defining the headings for the table, we move forward with the body section. The table body is defined within the <tbody> element. We create the rows using the <tr> element. Within each <tr> element, we enter the data or description for that row within the <td> element.

We create three rows within the body section of the table.

The output of the code is shown in Figure 5-10.

COMPANY	NAME OF THE REPRESENTATIVE	CITY
Fox Co.	Kobe Bryant	Los Angeles
Net Connections	Mike Jordan	Chicago
Hudson Bay Corp	Drake	Toronto

Figure 5-10. *Tables*

In Figure 5-10, we can see the table rows and columns displayed as explained in the code. You can also see a divider between the table rows owing to the divider class we used in the example.

You can create striped tables in UIkit. For that, you need to use the **uk-table-striped** class in conjunction with the **uk-table** class as shown in Listing 5-10.

Listing 5-10. Striped Tables

```
<table class="uk-table uk-table-striped">
    <thead>
        <tr style="background-color: Cyan;">
            <th><b>Company</b></th>
            <th><b>Name of the Representative</b></th>
            <th><b>City</b></th>
        </tr>
    </thead>
    <tbody>
        <tr>
            <td>Fox Co.</td>
            <td>Kobe Bryant</td>
            <td>Los Angeles</td>
        </tr>
        <tr>
            <td>Net Connections</td>
            <td>Mike Jordan</td>
            <td>Chicago</td>
        </tr>
        <tr>
            <td>Hudson Bay Corp</td>
            <td>Drake</td>
            <td>Toronto</td>
        </tr>
    </tbody>
</table>
```

In Listing 5-10, we have added the **uk-table-striped** class in conjunction with the **uk-table** class. The rest of the code is the same as that in the previous Listing 5-9, where we had defined normal tables.

The output of the code is shown in Figure 5-11.

COMPANY	NAME OF THE REPRESENTATIVE	CITY
Fox Co.	Kobe Bryant	Los Angeles
Net Connections	Mike Jordan	Chicago
Hudson Bay Corp	Drake	Toronto

Figure 5-11. *Zebra-striped styled tables*

In Figure 5-11, you can see a Zebra-striped styling applied to the rows of the tables.

You can also display a hover state for the table rows. For that, you need to add the **uk-table-hover** class to the table element as shown in Listing 5-11.

Listing 5-11. Hover functionality on tables

```
<table class="uk-table uk-table-divider uk-table-hover">
    <thead>
        <tr style="background-color: Cyan;">
            <th><b>Company</b></th>
            <th><b>Name of the Representative</b></th>
            <th><b>City</b></th>
        </tr>
    </thead>
    <tbody>
        <tr>
            <td>Fox Co.</td>
            <td>Kobe Bryant</td>
            <td>Los Angeles</td>
        </tr>
```

```
    <tr>
        <td>Net Connections</td>
        <td>Mike Jordan</td>
        <td>Chicago</td>
    </tr>
    <tr>
        <td>Hudson Bay Corp</td>
        <td>Drake</td>
        <td>Toronto</td>
    </tr>
    </tbody>
</table>
```

In Listing 5-11, we have added the **uk-table-hover** class in conjunction with the **uk-table** and **uk-table-divider** classes. The rest of the code is the same as in Listing 5-9 for normal tables.

The output of the code is shown in Figure 5-12 (on hovering over the first row).

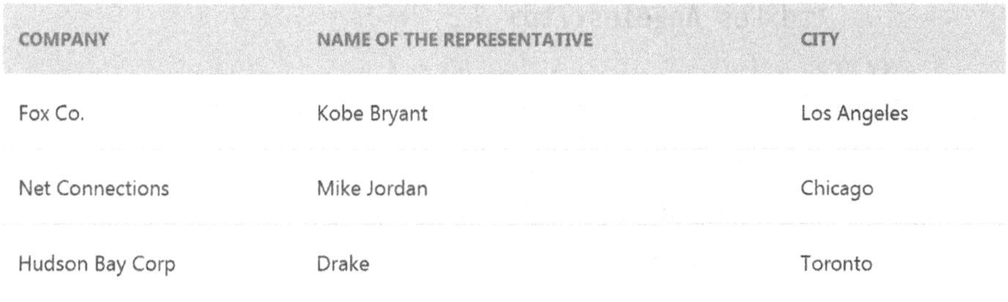

COMPANY	NAME OF THE REPRESENTATIVE	CITY
Fox Co.	Kobe Bryant	Los Angeles
Net Connections	Mike Jordan	Chicago
Hudson Bay Corp	Drake	Toronto

Figure 5-12. *Hover functionality*

The code on being executed will show the normal tables. When you hover over any row, it will result in a light yellow shade over that row highlighting it. As you can see, we have hovered over the first row as a result of which the first row is highlighted in a light yellow shade.

In UIkit, you can add size modifiers to increase or decrease the size of the tables. For that, you can add the **uk-table-large** or **uk-table-small** classes for large- and small-sized tables respectively. Let's see an illustration of a large-sized table in Listing 5-12.

Listing 5-12. Large-sized Table

```
<table class="uk-table uk-table-divider uk-table-large">
    <thead>
        <tr style="background-color: Cyan;">
            <th><b>Company</b></th>
            <th><b>Name of the Representative</b></th>
            <th><b>City</b></th>
        </tr>
    </thead>
    <tbody>
        <tr>
            <td>Fox Co.</td>
            <td>Kobe Bryant</td>
            <td>Los Angeles</td>
        </tr>
        <tr>
            <td>Net Connections</td>
            <td>Mike Jordan</td>
            <td>Chicago</td>
        </tr>
        <tr>
            <td>Hudson Bay Corp</td>
            <td>Drake</td>
            <td>Toronto</td>
        </tr>
    </tbody>
</table>
```

In Listing 5-12, we have added the **uk-table-large** class to the **uk-table** and **uk-table-divider** classes for the table element. The rest of the code is the same as that of the normal tables.

The output of the code is shown in Figure 5-13.

COMPANY	NAME OF THE REPRESENTATIVE	CITY
Fox Co.	Kobe Bryant	Los Angeles
Net Connections	Mike Jordan	Chicago
Hudson Bay Corp	Drake	Toronto

Figure 5-13. *Large-sized modified table*

In Figure 5-13, the table is relatively larger than the default table size as defined in the code.

You can center the table content vertically in UIkit. For that, you need to use the **uk-table-middle** class with the table element as shown in Listing 5-13.

Listing 5-13. Vertically-centered content alignment

```
<table class="uk-table uk-table-middle uk-table-divider">
    <thead>
        <tr style="background-color: Cyan;">
            <th><b>Company</b></th>
            <th><b>Name</b></th>
            <th><b>Work</b></th>
        </tr>
    </thead>
```

```
<tbody>
    <tr>
        <td>Fox Co.</td>
        <td>Drake</td>
        <td>Cat ipsum dolor sit amet, ea do or iste but
        corporis. Vitae laudantium for nequeporro dolores
        so velit. Adipisci lorem ipsa nulla odit laboris
        for nihil. Vitae ipsa laudantium eu amet. </td>
    </tr>
    <tr>
        <td>Maybach Group</td>
        <td>Rick Ross</td>
        <td>Cat ipsum dolor sit amet, ea do or iste but
        corporis. Vitae laudantium for nequeporro dolores
        so velit. Adipisci lorem ipsa nulla odit laboris
        for nihil. Vitae ipsa laudantium eu amet.</td>
    </tr>
        <tr>
        <td> Industrial Corp</td>
        <td>Prodigy</td>
        <td>Cat ipsum dolor sit amet, ea do or iste but
        corporis. Vitae laudantium for nequeporro dolores
        so velit. Adipisci lorem ipsa nulla odit laboris
        for nihil. Vitae ipsa laudantium eu amet. </td>
    </tr>
        <tr>
        <td> Alternative Holdings</td>
        <td>Chemical Brothers</td>
        <td>Cat ipsum dolor sit amet, ea do or iste but
        corporis. Vitae laudantium for nequeporro dolores
        so velit. Adipisci lorem ipsa nulla odit laboris
        for nihil. Vitae ipsa laudantium eu amet. </td>
```

```
        </tr>
     </tbody>
</table>
```

In Listing 5-13, we have used the **uk-table-middle** class in conjunction with the **uk-table** and **uk-table-divider** classes. The rest of the code structure is the same as normal tables except for the sample content and the description.

The output of the code is shown in Figure 5-14.

COMPANY	NAME	WORK
Fox Co.	Drake	Cat ipsum dolor sit amet, ea do or iste but corporis. Vitae laudantium for nequeporro dolores so velit. Adipisci lorem ipsa nulla odit laboris for nihil. Vitae ipsa laudantium eu amet.
Maybach Group	Rick Ross	Cat ipsum dolor sit amet, ea do or iste but corporis. Vitae laudantium for nequeporro dolores so velit. Adipisci lorem ipsa nulla odit laboris for nihil. Vitae ipsa laudantium eu amet.
Industrial Corp	Prodigy	Cat ipsum dolor sit amet, ea do or iste but corporis. Vitae laudantium for nequeporro dolores so velit. Adipisci lorem ipsa nulla odit laboris for nihil. Vitae ipsa laudantium eu amet.
Alternative Holdings	Chemical Brothers	Cat ipsum dolor sit amet, ea do or iste but corporis. Vitae laudantium for nequeporro dolores so velit. Adipisci lorem ipsa nulla odit laboris for nihil. Vitae ipsa laudantium eu amet.

Figure 5-14. *Vertically-centered content alignment*

In Figure 5-14, the content description is centered vertically as defined in the code.

At times, the tables are wider than the container width or are too large for a specific viewport. In that case, you need to wrap the table in a <div> container element and assign the **uk-overflow-auto** class to it as shown in Listing 5-14.

181

Listing 5-14. Table overflow responsiveness

```
<div class="uk-overflow-auto">
  <table class="uk-table uk-table-divider">
    <thead>
      <tr style="background-color: Cyan;">
        <th><b>Company</b></th>
        <th><b>Representative</b></th>
        <th><b>City</b></th>
        <th><b>Profession</b> </th>
        <th><b>League</b></th>
        <th><b>Year</b></th>
      </tr>
    </thead>
    <tbody>
      <tr>
        <td>Lakers</td>
        <td>Kobe Bryant</td>
        <td>Los Angeles</td>
        <td>Basketball</td>
        <td>NBA</td>
        <td>2000</td>
      </tr>
      <tr>
        <td>Supersonics</td>
        <td>Shawn Kemp</td>
        <td>Seattle</td>
        <td>Basketball</td>
        <td>NBA</td>
        <td>1995</td>
      </tr>
      <tr>
```

```
    <td>Jazz</td>
    <td>Karl Malone</td>
    <td>Utah</td>
    <td>Basketball</td>
    <td>NBA</td>
    <td>1995</td>
</tr>
<tr>
    <td>Suns</td>
    <td>Charles Barkley</td>
    <td>Phoenix</td>
    <td>Basketball</td>
    <td>NBA</td>
    <td>1995</td>
</tr>
<tr>
    <td>Bulls</td>
    <td>Mike Jordan</td>
    <td>Chicago</td>
    <td>Basketball</td>
    <td>NBA</td>
    <td>1995</td>
</tr>
<tr>
    <td>Raptors</td>
    <td>Chris Bosh</td>
    <td>Toronto</td>
    <td>Basketball</td>
    <td>NBA</td>
    <td>2004</td>
```

```
        </tr>
    </tbody>
</table>
```

In Listing 5-14, we have wrapped the table in a <div> parent container and assigned the **uk-overflow-auto** class to the parent <div> element. Then, we have defined a normal table similar to previous examples, except for the sample description - in addition, we have added more rows in the body section.

The output of the code on a tablet screen is shown in Figure 5-15.

COMPANY	REPRESENTATIVE	CITY	PROFESSION	LEAGUE
Lakers	Kobe Bryant	Los Angeles	Basketball	NBA
Supersonics	Shawn Kemp	Seattle	Basketball	NBA
Jazz	Karl Malone	Utah	Basketball	NBA
Suns	Charles Barkley	Phoenix	Basketball	NBA
Bulls	Mike Jordan	Chicago	Basketball	NBA
Raptors	Chris Bosh	Toronto	Basketball	NBA

Figure 5-15. *Responsiveness on table overflow*

In Figure 5-15, you can see that a horizontal scroll bar is introduced when the elements inside the table are wider than the tablet screen. This illustrates its responsiveness.

Summary

In this chapter, we learned about the different kinds of form elements in UIkit. We then created a Springer Sign-Up Form sample. Next, we learned about the different features and styling of Tables. In the next chapter, we will look as well as forecast some upcoming trends and tacks in the web design niche circa 2020.

CHAPTER 6

Web Design - Peek into the Upcoming Trends in 2020

Technology has grown leaps and bounds in today's fast-changing era, rendering the traditional methods of design redundant. ***Relevant Content is King*** has gained precedence over other facets of business. Moreover, considering the advent of data-driven analytics and Artificial Intelligence (AI), the rules of the game have changed significantly; it is all about information; accessibility to that data; deriving meaningful insights and implementing the essentials for better results, simultaneously using it for forecasting; and predictive modeling. While the archaic design practices were more focused on aesthetics and grandeur, the current digital age is increasingly leaning toward the ***function-over-form*** philosophy. Amplified uniformity, Easy consumption of information, Simplicity, Performance, and Usability are mission critical to design nowadays.

In this chapter, you will look at the different trends and possibilities that will be in vogue in 2020 (based on personal perception and viewpoint).

© Aravind Shenoy 2020
A. Shenoy, *Jumpstart UIKit*, https://doi.org/10.1007/978-1-4842-6029-6_6

Animations, Extensive Use of Colors, and Eye-Catching Typography

- Animations are going to be a pivotal facet in web design as they enable solid user engagement. Apart from being lively, they also help guide the users in an interactive way without the bulk or clutter. They are quite concise and drive the point effectively in addition to their aesthetic appeal.

- Pastel colors will be increasingly seen in web design, owing to their visual appeal. Moreover, websites and web apps tend to be more immersive with each passing day. Colors help define things in the way users perceive them. For example, the color blue defines depth or serenity, when you compare it to the ocean or the sky. They allocate a real-world experience to your sites/apps in line with the new-gen mindset, which is inclined toward more practicality. Even optimum use of colors in flat designs is likely to be prevalent in the future, a welcome change from the dull website flat designs observed in the past decade.

- Typography is moving toward bold fonts and different font styles that invoke user attention. They immediately denote that the sentence/words are important and help convey the message with the right impact. Apart from user-focus patterns, they also show immaculate readability in a no-frills way.

Mobile-Friendly Design

The contemporary millennial generation prefers high-fidelity mobile devices and smartphones to consume information on the web. On-the-go mobility and remote work facility anywhere, anytime, make the mobile phones the focal point of accessibility. Smartphone makers are coming out with a diverse range of devices, including cutting-edge utilities on a frequent basis. In the recent past, Google stated that mobile sites are the de facto choice compared to desktop versions of the sites.

Therefore, responsive web design is not an option anymore. From an SEO perspective, responsive sites are the way to go. In addition, mobile-first design is more or less the norm, wherein you build a site for the mobile platform and then enhance and tweak it for the desktop screens.

However, the settings are not set in stone as adaptive design is preferable in some cases, especially from a UX perspective, specifically tailored for a particular target audience.

Personally speaking, responsive web design is more relevant due to its future-proof pattern and the way web designing is evolving into digital design.

Progressive Web Apps

Recent studies advocate the use of web and mobile apps owing to their portability, offline accessibility, and prompt notifications. These apps work like client-server or web-based applications but are just websites in a compact form. Mobile apps take less time to build and facilitate seamless functioning alongside a high degree of credibility. Moreover, they can be customized significantly as per the target audience and business needs.

Agile Design Practices and Data-Driven Design

- In 2020, user experience will be essential for any vertical, including web design. Data-driven design is the future - you can implement the actionable insights you gain from advanced analytics. You can understand the high points, pain points, market trends, and also design predictive models. Coupled with next-gen AI analytics, data analysis can help you make viable decisions and drive more conversions. After all, analytics-driven practices ensure better decision-making, resulting in a satisfying user experience (also, think more like an end user and not just a designer/developer while creating websites).

- Agile web design and development is a combination of industry-best practices and frameworks, which enable enterprises to respond or create modern applications and UI layouts. Based on extensive collaboration and coordination, Agile methods are incremental in nature with excellent adaptability and predictability. Cross-functional teams work in tandem with each other, helping enterprises achieve faster delivery and tangible results. Agile methodologies are well equipped to deal with the latest technologies and design models, enabling timely inputs and modifications. The outcomes are essentially feasible and fully functional when compared to archaic design methods used in the past.

Flat Design

Keeping it simple is the adage today, especially relevant in the *function-over-form* philosophy (*Simple* & not *Simplified* ☺). There are several benefits of this minimalistic design principle as it helps designers adapt to change without any massive overhead. They also help users locate information easily and consume information better, while being SEO friendly. It also advocates optimal use of whitespace and helps design a clean interface without the bulk or clutter associated with complex layouts. Apart from taking the guesswork out, website loading speed is optimal in flat-design websites.

Emergence of Single-Page Websites

- 2020 will see several enterprises opting for a Single-Page application. Single-page applications/websites make it easier for the user to locate information. You just need to scroll down to the required section. Single-page design is mobile friendly and consistent across multiple devices/screen sizes.

- Single-page design has only internal links; therefore, the navigation is quite simpler and has more clarity. It is quite easier to design and maintain apart from being cost effective. Due to one long page only, you can derive more meaningful insights from Google Analytics and considerably optimize the website without any hassles.

- Bounce rates for single-page websites are quite low, and the conversions are higher compared to multipage websites.

Organic Illustrations

- While 2019 was all about geometric illustrations, natural and organic shapes are bound to rule the roost in 2020. For example, Material design is much more in use currently than ever before - users are likely to root for real-world shapes, something they can relate to instead of unreal geometric shapes. Also, hand-drawn or 3D digital graphics will be in vogue in the coming years. As web design is set to converge into digital design, the future is all about creating an immersive user experience.

- There has been a decline in the use of Flash in the past years. The year 2020 will see the inevitable demise of Flash, especially with Adobe offering no more updates or enhancements for Flash Players. HTML5 is predominantly used to replace Flash due to the high degree of uniformity across all device types.

Chat-bots

Chat-bots are increasingly becoming a common feature in websites today. For example, e-commerce websites have chat-bots for initial interaction (think *online chat support*) with the customers. Recently, it has been observed that chat-bots address the customer concerns effectively and only escalate the customer concerns to a customer care executive as per the requirements or resolution procedures. Apart from time and cost savings, they depict more of a round-the-clock support for customer, an important aspect in ensuring a fulfilling consumer experience.

Therefore, 2020 will incline toward chat-bots becoming a regular feature in most websites, especially in the services industry. Chat-bot adoption is sure to grow manifold and will be crucial while designing UIs in the coming decade.

Accessibility

- Accessibility should encompass all types of users, even those with disabilities of any nature. In the future (not just 2020), accessibility will not have the current limitations - accessibility for people with disabilities will be more of a mandatory inclusion and vital to any design.

- When it comes to accessibility, a new trend in websites is to provide the facility of one-click sign-in. It helps tackle the frequent login issues and improves user engagement, leading to more conversions. Empowering site users to access their data/information with a single-click accounts for an exceptional user experience.

Voice Search

Google, Amazon, and Apple have pushed forward the case of the Voice Search paradigm. In the near future, Voice Search will be more prevalent than ever owing to its coherent capabilities to increase conversions, relevancy, and more personalization. Comprehensive Feature Snippets,

Long tail Keywords, and optimal Site speed will be critical factors in aiding voice search. AI-powered implementation will also play a major role in site optimization in years to come.

- When it comes to web design, you can place featured snippets containing the relevant data in the header or navigation components. As Voice Search is more inclined toward localization, you can add content, visuals, videos, and images based on the relevant location. An example would be registering your business in Google Local for distinctive visibility.

- You can mark long tail phrases in your structured data and metadata. Another excellent way of highlighting vital information is by using them in callouts and panels on your website. It grabs user attention and is easy to locate. (*Tip - Google Analytics is quite powerful and helps find the conversational type of search terms and phrases for your business niche.*)

- Mobile phones are the preferred media for voice searches. Mobile responsiveness is crucial while designing your site for Voice search. Therefore, Mobile-first or Mobile-friendly design is just right for creating and optimizing your sites for voice search.

- Voice searches abstract the need to type and scroll, specifically enabling frictionless hands-free interactions. Once users give voice input, they expect the results to be faster than the traditional way of typing search queries for obtaining information. So, page loading speed has to be faster – therefore, site optimization for site speed is a given.

- Video marketing is increasingly being used on sites as they gather more traction compared to old ways of marketing. When it comes to voice search, designers should customize the site design to incorporate precise and detailed transcripts for videos.

Summary

In today's digitized world, web designers are morphing into digital designers. The fundamentals of site/app design have changed considerably with data and analytics being the focal points. In the current times, web design is not focused on aesthetics only - instead, the focus is more on ease of use, interactive attributes, readability, and accessibility. The target audience is the crux of digital platforms.

Real-time methodologies in web design are pan-optic in nature. As websites have a lot of dynamic features, usability is the core. UX designers will work in conjunction with web designers to chalk out many wireframes and prototypes before arriving at the final design. Data-driven development will prove to be a game-changing methodology in the UI design and development life cycle.

A website nowadays is your first point of communication for your enterprise with the business world. So, the future is as much about user interaction as it is about the look and feel of sites. A total approach may involve comprehending the digital space with a macroscopic perspective, a world in itself to explore. To infer, web design is inclined toward a unified viewpoint, concentrated on empowering enterprises with that competitive edge in this digital age, opening up a world of possibilities.

Thank You ☺

Index

A

Accessibility, 193
Accordions, 113–116
Adaptive design *vs.* Responsive
    web design, 4–6
Agile web design/development, 190
Animations, 188

B

Breadcrumbs, 77–78
Buttons (CSS/JavaScript)
    contextual colors, 105–106
    groups, 108–109
    normal button, 104–105
    small and large-sized
        buttons, 106
    width modifiers, 107–108

C

Carousel slider, 90–96
Cascading Style Sheets (CSS)
    accordions, 113–116
    animation, 146–150
    buttons, 104–109
    components, 103

contextual alert boxes, 116–120
icons library
    CDN icon library script, 109
    normal icons, 110
    ratio modifiers, 110–111
    social media buttons, 112
inverse component, 137–140
modals
    full-width, 125–126
    images/videos, 127–128
    normal modals, 122–125
padding component, 135
pagination, 143–145
panel component, 128–130
responsive classes, 141
tile component, 131–135
tooltips, 120–122
transition component, 150–153
upload functionality, 137–139
visibility classes, 140–143
Chat-bots, 192–193
Containers
    border radius, 46–48
    box shadows, 48–50
    concepts, 41
    different-size allocation, 42–44
    drop cap feature, 50–51

© Aravind Shenoy 2020
A. Shenoy, *Jumpstart UIKit*, https://doi.org/10.1007/978-1-4842-6029-6

Containers (*cont.*)
   float/clearfix, 45–46
   inclusive component, 42
   section class, 41
   sized elements, 44
   text/image logos, 51–52
   utility classes, 45
Content Delivery
   Network (CDN), 9
Content management
   systems (CMS), 4
Contextual alert
   boxes, 116–120
Contextual-colored
   buttons, 105–106

D, E

Data-driven design, 190

F

Flat-design websites, 191
Forms
   contextual colors, 157–160
   grid-width layouts, 161–162
   horizontal labels, 168
   icons, 164–166
   input textboxes, 156, 168
   select options, 162–164
   sign-up form, 169–172
   stacked labels, 166–168
   tables (*see* Tables)
   utilities, 155

G, H

Geometric illustrations, 192
Grid System
   auto/expand class
      implementation, 21–22
   child elements, 19
   code output, 20
   column class, 40
   component, 17
   fixed widths applying, 22
   flexbox power layouts, 16
   flex feature, 32–35
   fractions, 17
   gap modifiers, 24–26
   grid-fixed widths, 22
   individual row/column, 27, 28
   item repositioning, 39
   length/columns spanning, 16
   match utility, 29–30
   nested grids, 30–31
   pre-defined implementation, 24
   vertical columns, 35–36
   width, 16
   wrap/wrap-around utility, 37–39
Grouped buttons, 108–109

I

Icon navigation, 79–81

J, K

JavaScript, *see* Cascading Style
   Sheets (CSS)

L

List navigations
    active class, 61–62
    divider class, 63–64
    nested navigation
        elements, 64–66
    primary modifier, 62–63
    uk-active class, 61

M

Media attributes
    badges, 88
    carousel slider, 90–96
    labels, 87–88
    slideshow, 95–102
Mobile-friendly design, 189
Modals
    full-width, 125–126
    images/videos, 127–128
    normal modals
        attribute activation, 123–124
        header/body/
          footer, 122–123
        overlay, 124–125

N

Navigation elements
    animation effect, 59
    breadcrumbs, 77–78
    components, 55
    dropdown, 56–60
    icon navigation, 79–81
    list navigations, 61–66
    media attributes (*see* Media
        attributes)
    navbar design, 70–77
    sub navigation, 81–83
    tabs-based
        navigation, 66–70
    thumbnail navigation, 83–87
Navjs jQuery file, 74

O

Organic illustrations, 192

P, Q

Pastel colors, 188
Progressive web apps, 189

R

Ratio modifiers icons, 110
Responsive web design
    vs. adaptive design, 4
    evolution, 1
    function-over-form
        approach, 5
    innumerable testing, 2
    intuitive approach, 3–5
    mobile platform, 2, 3
    pivotal factor, 3
    responsive web design, 2
    web addresses, 2

S

Single-page application, 191
Slideshow
    animation scale feature, 98
    component, 96
    executing code, 97
    feature, 95–102
    Kenburns effect, 100
    scaling effect, 99
    zooming effect, 101–102
Social media icon buttons, 112
Sub navigation, 81–83

T

Tables
    Hover function, 176–177
    large-sized table, 178–179
    normal tables, 173–174
    overflow responsiveness,
        182–184
    source code, 174
    striped creation, 174
    vertically-centered
        content, 179–181
    zebra-striped style, 176

Tabs-based navigation, 66–70
Thumbnail navigation, 83–87
Tooltips, 120–122
Transition component, 150–153
Typography, 188

U

UIkit web application
    benefits, 9
    CDN links, 8
    commands, 9
    dependencies, 9–10
    desktop website, 6
    file structure, 11
    evolution (*see* Responsive
        web design)
    file structure, 8
    mobile site, 5–6
    red box download, 7
    starter template, 14–15
    website, 5

V, W, X, Y, Z

Voice search paradigm, 193–195